The Postmodern Political Condition

The Postmodern Political Condition

Agnes Heller and Ferenc Fehér

New York
Columbia University Press

Copyright © Agnes Heller and Ferenc Fehér 1988

Printed in Great Britain

Casebound editions of Columbia University Press books are printed on
permanent and durable acid-free paper.

Library of Congress Cataloging-in-Publication Data
Heller, Agnes.
   The postmodern political condition.
   Includes index.
   1. Political ethics. 2. Political science—Philosophy.
  3. Postmodernism. I. Fehér, Ferenc, 1928– .
  II. Title
  JA79.H45 1989   172   88–35284
  ISBN 0–231–07022–5 (alk. paper)

Contents

Acknowledgements

The authors and publisher would like to thank the following for permission to use material previously published elsewhere:

Agnes Heller, 'The Moral Situation in Modernity', *Social Research*, New York, Vol. 55 No. 4, Winter 1988;
Ference Feher, 'The Pariah and the Citizen', *Thesis Eleven*, Melbourne, No. 15, 1986;
Agnes Heller, 'Existentialism, Alienation, Postmodernism', published in French, 'Les mouvements culturels', *Lettre Internationale*, Paris, No. 15, Winter 1987;
Agnes Heller, 'Europe – An Epilogue?' published in French 'L'Europe, un epilogue?' *Lettre Internationale*, No. 18, Fall 1988.

1

The Postmodern Political Condition

Postmodernity is neither a historical period nor a cultural or political trend with well-defined characteristics. Rather, postmodernity may be understood as the private-collective time and space, within the wider time and space of modernity, delineated by those who have problems with and queries addressed to modernity, by those who want to take it to task, and by those who make an inventory of modernity's achievements as well as its unresolved dilemmas. Those who have chosen to dwell in postmodernity nevertheless live among moderns as well as premoderns. For the very foundation of postmodernity consists of viewing the world as a plurality of heterogeneous spaces and temporalities. Postmodernity thus can only define itself within this plurality, against these heterogeneous others.

Our main political and cultural dilemma, in so far as we have designated ourselves as postmodern, is captured by the vagueness of the term 'post' itself. Today's thinking is replete with categories whose *differentia specifica* is provided by this prefix. For example, we now have 'post-structuralism', 'post-industrial' and 'post-revolutionary' societies, even *post-histoire*. Thus, the primary concern of those living the present as postmodern is that they live in the present while at the same time, both temporally as well as spatially, they are *being after*.

Politically speaking, those who have chosen to understand themselves as postmodern are in the first place after 'the grand narrative'. The grand narrative, not to be confused with holism, which is, according to Lyotard, conducive to totalitarianism, is world interpretation of a very peculiar kind. It is best summarized by Gauguin's famous question: where did we come from, what are we, where are going? The grand narrative has therefore a fixed point of origin normally enlarged into mythological dimensions and given such symbolic weight that the story can subsequently be read only *ab urbe condita*. The grand narrative recounts the story with an overtly causal, covertly teleological self-confidence. This position of superiority to the recounted story implies a philosophical and political transcendentalism, the presence of the omiscient narrator. The latter is apparently *au-dessus-de-la-mêlée*, while in fact the narrator, like a deity in an epic poem, takes sides with one protagonist and paralyses another. As a rule, the grand narrative 'unconceals' its telos at the end, a telos which had been first posited along with the invention of the origin. But those dwelling in the postmodern political condition feel themselves to be after the entire story with its sacred and mythological origin, strict causality, secret teleology, omniscient and transcendent narrator and its promise of a happy ending in a cosmic or historic sense.

Our further political concern, when we choose to call ourselves 'postmodern', is the process in which 'Europe' is gradually becoming a museum. The project termed 'Europe' has always been the hermeneutical culture *par excellence*. This inherent hermeneutical character has created a peculiar internal tension in the project since time immemorial. On the one hand, 'Europe' had always been more expansive and more expressly universalistic than other cultural projects. Europeans did not merely understand their culture as superior to others and these alien others as inferior to them. They also believed that the 'truth' of European culture is in the same measure the as-yet-hidden truth (and telos) of other cultures, but that time had not yet come for the latter to realize it. On the other hand, Europeans had been regularly subjecting their own culture to inquiries into their putative universals, to expose them as just so many particularities having a false claim to universality. The meaning of the concept 'ideology' had appeared in this culture *avant la lettre*. In exposing the particularity of all European universals and in proceeding from here towards the creation of the most universal universals, Marx only proved to be the ultimate European. At some point the time had to come when Europeans were bound to question the project 'Europe' as a whole; when they had to expose the false claim of universality inherent in the 'European particular'. The cultural and political campaign against ethnocentrism has in fact been a major campaign *for* postmodernity.

The otherwise misty term 'post-structuralism' also has a political meaning in post-modernity: it indicates the social and political prevalence of the functional over the structural, the gradual weakening, if not total disappearance of, a politics based solely on class interests and class perceptions. This statement is not an assertion of (non-existing) social harmony in today's western society. Rather it is a comment upon the character of its internal conflicts. The traditional social collisions, mostly economic in nature, remain virulent in all inconsistently welfarist countries or in countries where a neo-conservative trend tends to weaken the welfarist character of society. Above all, state and trade unions are bitterly enmeshed in them, and violent economic conflicts between state and class-based organizations characterize modern politics *sui generis*. However, alongside the mainstream, unmistakable trends of postmodern politics emerge both on the right and the left which are function-based and function-targeted in a double sense. They are, in the first place, aiming at the strengthening or elimination respectively of a single function of modernity. These are the movements which overwhelmingly appear as single-issue actions and which are the epitomes of functionalist-postmodern politics. Secondly, once again both on the right and the left, there are more general attempts at rearranging the given network of functions in a particular society. The trends and upheavals in today's politics simply cannot be understood in modernist-class categories, for their interpretation in strictly structural (class) terms would lead to absurd results. Paradigmatic examples of such post-modernist-functionalist trends are Thatcher's project of a 'popular capitalism' on the extreme right end of the political spectrum and May 1968 in Paris on the radical-leftist end. (The latter was at any rate characterised by 'false consciousness' of a peculiar type. While it was in fact targeted on function and on the rearrangement of functionality, it still conducted a structuralist discourse of the 'new working class'. It also understood itself of the grand narrative as being about 'the end of alienation'.) 'Being after', therefore, means in this sense, 'being after the class scenarios'.

'Being after', this dominant life-feeling of postmodernity, generates a special political emphasis about the present (as well as about the 'past-of-the-present' and 'future-of-the-present') which is, short of a nuclear catastrophe, our sole eternity. *Post-histoire* as the dominant temporality of the postmodern condition is a surprising vindication of Hegel's political philosophy, his celebrated thesis of the reconciliation with reality. This philosophy, unexpectedly, turns out to be yet another conception of *post-histoire* in its final outcome: there had been History before Hegel's philosophy, and the 'homecoming of the World Spirit', but there is no longer. Rather, all our political tasks mapped out in *The Philosophy of Right* rest precisely on this present stage of *post-histoire*. Hegel viewed the latter with no enthusiasm at all, rather with a bitter and disillusioned realism, yet he certainly did not regard it as an age of banality unworthy of consideration by political philosophy.

The dominant temporality of post-modernity has serious political implications as well. Redemptive politics of any kind are incompatible with the postmodern political condition. For Messianic claims and expectations mean infinitely more than merely the questioning and taking to task of modernity which is the self-adopted task of postmodernity. The postmodern self-limitation to the present as our one and only eternity also excludes experiments with 'leaps into *nihil*', that is, attempts at the *absolute* transcendence of modernity. At the same time, the postmodern political condition is tremendously ill at ease with Utopianism of even a non-Messianic type, which makes it vulnerable to easy compromises with the present as well as susceptible to 'doomsday myths' and collective fears stemming from the loss of future.

The 'recycling of theories' (or political solutions) is an equally characteristic feature of the postmodern political condition. This feature is anchored in *post-histoire*. For at least one implication of the term is tantamount to attempts to repossess all histories, all past and seemingly extinct wisdoms and collective efforts barred from us either by the possessive parent, Europe, or by the spirit of modernity craving for what is *de dernier cri*. Prior to postmodernity, our political language was as replete with prophecies about 'end-and-no-return' as with the prefix 'post'. In close sequence, we have lived through the 'end of ideology', the 'end of religion', the 'end of Marxism', the 'end of scientificity' and the 'end of evolutionism'. Yet there are definite indications that in postmodern temporality none of these areas have been lost beyond retrieval. The merry-go-round of 'eternally lost' and later retrieved theories and practices is of course not tantamount to the religious aura of resurrection. And yet, we can detect a powerful need behind the recycling: our constant quest for roots in the postmodern condition, a non-holistic quest which as a rule lifts isolated and valued efforts of the past out of their context and leaves the framework behind. The reason why 'recycling' is not perforce conducive to absolute relativism is that the postmodern political condition also serves as a filter and a limit in rejecting the grand narrative. The ideas and collective practices which are the most unlikely to be recycled (although not even their temporary retrieval is absolutely excluded) are built on the strongest grand narrative.

The postmodern political condition is premissed on the acceptance of the plurality of cultures and discourses. Pluralism (of various kinds) is implicit in postmodernity as a project. The breakdown of the grand narrative is a direct invitation to cohabitation amongst various (local, cultural, ethnic, religious, 'ideological') small narratives. Their co-existence, however, can take on extremely different forms. It may appear as the totally relativistic indifference of respective cultures to one another. It may become manifest as the thoroughly inauthentic adoration of 'the other' (the 'third-worldism' of first-world intellectuals). It can be accompanied by the total denial, as well as by the relativization, of universals. The meaning of the total rejection of universalism is self-evident. It should be noted, however, that 'holistic anti-universalism' (a highly contradictory position on its own terms) is coupled with two further negative terms: philosophical 'anti-humanism' and with a specific interpretation of *post-histoire* in which the term means the negation, and not just the end, of history. Postmodernist 'anti-humanism', which is fully exhibited in a typical reception of Heidegger and Derrida, may not necessarily conclude in a philosophical *plaidoyer* for barbarism (although it is constantly exposed to this danger). It may simply assert, in a philosophically correct way, that the cluster termed 'humankind' has so far attained to no common substrate and it is therefore not much more than a semi-religious 'mana' which we can re-live in music but which cannot be turned into the pragmatic matter of political action. However, philosophical anti-humanism *ipso facto* implies the total rejection of (political) universalism. In a similar fashion, the interpretation of *post-histoire* as the negation of history not only denies the Hegelian *Universalgeschichte* (with its common substrate, rules and laws). It also reduces history to the mere dimension of temporality, the mere aggregate of events in temporality or cluster which in itself is meaningless. The sociological conclusion to be drawn from this premiss is the understanding of the social as an 'artefact'. This seemingly innocent sociological issue can, however, become the theoretical grounding for political arbitrariness and authoritarianism of various kinds (as well as serving as a sufficient explanation for the sudden renaissance of the political theory of Carl Schmitt.) However, the relativization of universalism can also provide a solid foundation for the (Habermasian) 'domination-free' discourse between various cultures. The latter departs from a dual premiss: from the philosophical critique of the concept 'humanism' (together with the recognition of the need for its existence, which becomes manifest in the 'mana' of humanism) *and* from registering common, or at least similar, trends in various cultures. This commonness or similarity is the potential of later (relative) generalizations and universalizations.

A major factor furthering the relative universalism of the postmodern condition is the fact that there is no longer *terra incognita* in our political geography. The collapse of the colonial system (together with the subsequent qualms of white conscience) as well as the 'museification of Europe' have closed the long period of unashamed cultural supremacy on a note of 'the quest for the primitive', to use a well-known anthropological term. The so-called 'third world' has been sharply, sometimes in a positive, sometimes in a negative sense, engraved on the membrane of the consciousness of 'the first world'. Nor is Soviet society a 'mystery wrapped up in an enigma' as it still was for Churchill's generation. It is increasingly understood as the frightening and menacing continuation and intensification of certain trends inherent in the west. And recently astute observers of the Soviet system have detected unmistakable signs of postmodernism in the discourse of the dissidents.

The breakdown of the grand narrative of secularization is a fact of the postmodern political condition, which is backed by a plethora of empirical evidence and by the widespread, and widely pluralistic, religious revival from 'right-to-life' – campaigners to liberation theologians. Secularization, this 'religion of the atheist', was without doubt one of the representative grand narratives of the political scene after the French Revolution. It thrived on the ruins of the first failed attempts at building a 'civil religion'; a new, revolutionary religion which either compromised itself by degrading into a terroristic state doctrine, or which never succeeded in transcending the narrow confines of a private-sectarian realm. Secularization can indeed be termed without the verbal excesses of journalism, the civil religion of the atheist, for it implies a strict (albeit negative) creed and it holds out such redemptive promises as making society fully transparent, creating a paradise on earth, compensating for the limited duration of human life and the like. In addition, in several countries it has become the dominant, internalized, occasionally even institutionalized, ethos. The major postmodernist feature of the present religious revival consists in the fact that the new cycle of spontaneous religious fervour is deeply pluralistic, often ecumenical and is therefore full of hybrid phenomena. (One such revival, which firmly intends to remain within traditional Catholicism, but which at the same time frontally challenges fundamental aspects of the dogma, as for example, the Pope's infallibility, can only be termed 'Catholic Protestantism'.) These new breeds of postmodernist devotion are not generating chiliastic expectations. They are rather 'secular religions' in the sense of focusing on the religious-model regulation of the private sphere. For the most part, metaphysically they are indifferent and, in this sense, pluralistic, sometimes up to the point of 'anything goes'. This loosely relativistic-pluralistic religious upheaval might turn out to be a new 'ruse of reason' in proving to be the conclusive action of a long quest for genuine religious tolerance. In so far as the inherent 'Protestantism' of *all* its branches erodes Church authority, and the social progressiveness of several of its branches weakens the zeal of the surviving contingents of the atheist 'civil religion', they might significantly contribute to achieving the age-old dream: a world in which religious belief is truly a private issue and its underpinning, metaphysics, an individual vision of the world. However, a collateral, and dangerous, phenomenon has to be emphasized here: the equally emerging religious (and secular) fundamentalism. The new fundamentalism is the voice of the bad conscience of the postmodern condition flagellating itself for its excessive indulgence in relativism. The new religious and secular fundamentalism (which, as far as their main features are concerned, run along very similar lines and sometimes coalesce) does not offer a novel grand narrative; it is much too postmodern for this. Fundamentalists rather select one aspect of the dogma, one 'text of foundation' with regard to which they declare all attempts at hermeneutics politically subversive. (More recently, Dworkin has analysed in a very convincing manner that the underlying philosophical-political issue behind the political drama around the nomination of Judge Bork to the United States Supreme Court was precisely his fundamentalist intolerance towards a hermeneutics of the Constitution.)

Postmodernity has in every respect including the political, a double face like Janus. The weakening, and occasionally disappearance, of class scenarios and the ascendency of the functionalist character of society has contributed enormously to the rearrangement and 'modernization' of traditional political patterns and programmes. The habitual understanding of the state as a mere 'class agency' had to be replaced by more sophisticated conceptions when the 'class against class' line-up in the political arena ceded ground to much more complex recipes. This reconceptualization in turn contributed to taking the state, and above all the democratic institutions, incomparably more seriously than had ever happened on the left. The vanishing or drastic transformation of west-European communism (which exists only in name) is in the main due to the weakening of the class scenarios and its theoretical consequences. The shifting proportions of political significance from parties toward movements (a process which on the whole is tantamount to the European assimilation of American political habits, a new pattern in terms of which movements rather than parties forge the political options) also results from, or at least has been largely facilitated by, the reduced role of classes and class strategies. However, a crucial feature of western politics in the last two hundred years has been significantly eroded by the same change: its rationality. True enough, whatever sublime universalist role has been attributed to various classes by ideologues, in reality classes and class strategies have always been egoistic in so far as they were interest-motivated. But politics based on interest have one eminent rational propensity: they are calculable and as such more or less predictable. In this respect the yield of the postmodern condition is almost entirely negative in so far as politics and political change have become almost totally irrational and unpredictable. The relative share of nationalism, a factor of invariably dubious rationality, has remained a constant, to say the least. Its share has perhaps been increased. What is worse, its function has changed. For there is a great deal of truth in the old Marxist truism, that the 'national question' had been, up until the foundation of the modern nation states, a class issue to a very great extent. Once, however, the nation states had come about, the emphasis on the national component, so much on display in the postmodern political condition, heightened the irrational element in postmodern politics. Racism, which one would have believed dead after Hitler, became a politicized issue again, and this is not entirely unrelated to postmodern relativism which has undermined our sense of taboo. The 'ethnicity component' of politics, which seemed to have been wiped out by the existence of the nation state, has become once again an explosive conflict.

A special mention is due to the changing role of the students' movements in this increasingly irrational and unpredictable atmosphere of postmodern politics. Despite the fact that retrospectively one can clearly observe much self-delusion in a prominent collective social actor, it seems to us an incontrovertible fact that the students' movement had the lion's share in the great emancipatory deeds of the sixties: in fighting for civil rights and bringing the war machine to a halt in the United States, as well as in promoting the functionalist change in Europe (albeit their explicit and heavily ideological objectives were entirely different.) However, already in the sixties the warning signal could be seen in the movement of the Chinese students. For they prepared the ground for, as well as engineered, one of the major political catastrophes of our time after World War Two: the 'cultural revolution'. A similar political drama of almost comparable magnitude unfolded in Iran, where the students of the overplanned and overgrown University of Tehran served as pretorians for Khomeini's dictatorship.

The left has made several 'sophisticated' attempts since the sixties to redeem these movements (above all in China) and to give these events a 'philosophical' interpretation which would have related them to issues like the 'abolition of the division of labour'. We are convinced, however, that these movements only produced unmitigated devastation, instead of yielding philosophical lessons, and that these catastrophes were in the main due to the irrationality of postmodern politics, the precursors of which in many respects they were. Students as a separate social group have legitimate group interests of their own, as students in the present, and as a new contingent of the administrators of organized knowledge, the intelligentsia, in the future. In so far as they defend such interests and critically dissect the anatomy of the academia and the like, they do not fulfil Messianic and philosophical functions, but they do pursue rational political activity irrespective of its merits. (It was a reassuring sign of the common sense of both American and French student politics that, as has been strongly emphasized by Alain Touraine, they were not targeted to mythological objectives but focused on the highly rational demand of modernizing the academia and society as a whole.) However, in those countries where class structure was anyhow only in the making or where violent revolutions had destroyed and ideologically confused class relations and class issue, it was easy to cross the Rubicon between modern and postmodern politics. This is why it was in these regions of the world that students embarked on destructive social experiments in which group (or class) interests played a negligible role (except the egoistic interest of those small sections of the movement which aimed at the seizure of power and at the change of elite). In this highly negative sense, 'backward' countries had become for once preceptors of so-called 'developed' ones. What remains to be seen is whether the latter have indeed learned the lesson.

We are witnessing the same Janus-faced relationship between politics and morality as is evident in every other aspect of the postmodern political condition. If total moral relativism, which is undeniably one of the options of postmodernity, gains the upper hand, even the assessment of mass deportation and genocide becomes a matter of taste. (That this is more than a theoretical possibility is proven by Le Pen's 'postmodern fascism'. For Le Pen, the Holocaust, about which he stylishly pleads agnosticism, if it had indeed happened, is a minor issue whose evaluation depends on a more general interpretation of methods of warfare.) However, the postmodern political condition also has certain positive potentials, which can best be summed up by Adorno's famous term: *minima moralia*. Although generally speaking the atmosphere of the postmodern political condition is not conducive to universals, moral discourse is nevertheless still going on in its niches and *intermundia*. From such discourses (in the plural) certain moral principles of democratic politics can indeed be extracted, and this book will consist of an attempt at formulating them.

Economic issues are also prominent in the postmodern political condition, again both in a positive as well as negative sense. The positive side of the coin is that both conservative and radical myths of the 'social question' have been worn thin in the last decades. After what seems to be the longest, if certainly not the stormiest, depressive cycle of capitalist economy, hardly anyone entertains high hopes of the perennial and uninterrupted existence of the 'affluent society'. However, simultaneously with the demise of the liberal myth, the leftist myth of 'solving the social question' *in toto* and for good has also been considerably eroded. Among others, the pluralism of the postmodern condition also manifests itself in the continuous creation of brand-new, and highly diverse, social issues, and in this process the solution of an old issue is the precondition of the birth of a new one. We are still very far from universal recognition of the inescapable conclusion that the complete solution of the 'social question' is either a myth or a regulative idea. However, the inherent pluralism of the postmodern condition is the ideal atmosphere in which such a recognition can be achieved. The negative aspect of the present situation concerns a problematic division of labour between parties and movements. In the last decades in western politics parties have almost exclusively become economic agencies while movements have been allotted the role of forging the political options. As a result, elections are focusing, almost without exception, on economic issues. And while we disagree with Hannah Arendt's famous thesis that the social should be banned from the political arena, and we attribute a great importance to movements, the prevalence of economic issues in professional politics is a dubious result.

Is what we term the 'postmodern political condition' a new period of politics? We have to reiterate what has been suggested from the outset: postmodernity (including the postmodern political condition) is not a new era. Postmodernity is in every respect 'parasitic' on modernity; it lives and feeds on its achievements and on its dilemmas. What *is* new in the situation is the novel historical consciousness developed in *post-histoire*; the spreading feeling that we are permanently going to be in the present and, at the same time, after it. With the same gesture, we have appropriated our present more profoundly than we had ever done, as well as developed a critical distance from it. And whoever remains dissatisfied with only this amount of critical distance from our political perspectives should bear in mind that an absolute negation of the present (which is undeniably more than could be offered by postmodernity) would in all probability end either in a total loss of freedom or in total destruction. And both outcomes would be more than, or rather different from, the postmodern. They would be thoroughly antimodernist.

The thesis of 'the postmodern political condition' argued for in the chapters of this book is the result of the authors' sometimes solitary, sometimes collective pondering of the political scene in the last three or four years. The first signal that triggered the reconsideration of our political vocabulary was the recent conspicuous breaking down of 'grand narratives'. The protracted, increasingly sterile, debates about 'the crisis of Marxism,' and later the considerably more stimulating controversies about various 'micro-discourses', the perception of a fragmented religious revival, the understanding of the necessity of an *incomplete* concept of ethico-political justice (elaborated in full detail in Agnes Heller's book, *Beyond Justice*) – all these new developments indicated to us 'the end of the grand narrative'. This being so, generalizations about modernity, and the constant quest for, and discovery of, new universal tendencies had to be either abandoned or at least more cautiously stated. Chapter 2, which deals with satisfaction in a dissatisfied society, is proof of this methodological caution. 'Dissatisfaction', a trend observed by Weber, is a more or less general-universal feature of modernity. However, the assumption that 'dissatisfaction' is the necessary characteristic of modernity which appears simultaneously in all its facets and levels, a trend universally present in all its periods and one which extends over its whole socio-political map, now seems to us an exaggeration. The dominant trend of the postmodern condition rather tolerates, even promotes, significant niches of satisfaction in various forms within individual or collective life strategies. And such niches represent more than mere 'cultural monasteries' or exceptions to the rule. They increasingly become constitutive features of modernity in the absence of which we can hardly conceive of modernity's survival. For the ideology and practice of universal dissatisfaction is fuelled by, and it in turn fuels, a cycle of unstoppable growth, which is increasingly disruptive of the conditions of modern life.

The main thrust of our inquiry into 'the postmodern political condition' is not confined to merely registering the emerging new heterogeneity of modernity, a heterogeneity which can hardly, or only forcibly, be homogenized by the surviving, seriously flawed 'grand narratives'. Instead we embark on a quest for the ties which are still capable of holding our world together, for an ethos which, we surmise, might have outlived the process of fragmentation and which could serve as an antidote to the cynicism of absolute relativism. In short, we try to ascertain how much universalism remains even in the postmodern political condition. In penetrating this apparent lacuna, behind which we persistently try to bring to light existing ties, we focus on the *post-modern political ethos* and its preconditions. Methodologically speaking, this means targeting not discursive-decisionist issues, but rather the preconditions of an ongoing political discourse. In this sense, we would characterize *The Postmodern Political Condition* as an exercise in political philosophy.

The message of the book can be captured in two questions. The first reads as follows: 'what are the dangers threatening the lifeline of modernity, the democratic-liberal as well as 'democratic socialist' traditions, values, legacies, institutions and aspirations in the 'postmodern political condition'? The second question: 'how can these traditions, trends and aspirations not only be redeemed but also further developed?' As a result of these focuses, the issues of a new civic ethics and civic virtues, those of reformulating social norms, the problems of political decision-making and social justice were placed at the centre of our project. Due to this shift in interest which this represented for us, the habitual debates of modern political theory, for example the controversy between 'the revolutionary' and 'the reformist' positions, have faded from our vision seeming to lack relevance. At the same time, somewhat neglected political theories, for example Hannah Arendt's analyses of the 'republic', 'the citizen', 'the act of foundation as *constitutio libertatis*' have gained in significance for us.

An issue central to Habermas' theory, namely that of *consensus*, is also important for us but not as the organizing centre of our political inquiry and philosophy. This is so, firstly, because we heed Arendt's warning about the potentially totalitarian and oppressive character of consensus politics. Behind this issue is a major complex combining the rules of democratic procedure, whether parliamentary or direct-participatory or both, with substantive liberal values and vetoes, an aspect which already had been singled out by Benjamin Constant as the specifically modern instance of liberty in contrast to the freedom of the ancient. Secondly, in *The Postmodern Political Condition* we focus on the fragmentation of universals and therefore on factors which hinder rather than facilitate consensus. But since our aim is the reconstitution of the unity of modernity to whatever degree possible within the postmodern political condition, we emphasize the crucial importance of social, cultural and political movements in our analysis. One can be seriously critical of the political strategies of various movements, and indeed we have criticized particular movements for what we have regarded as their political illusions. However, to turn a blind eye to their constitutive role in socio-political and cultural changes in the post-World-War-Two political scene is to remain inaccessible to the novelty of the postmodern political condition.

The postmodern political condition is fundamentally a European innovation and politico-cultural creation. However, it has been embraced in non-European worlds (above all in the United States) or at least in worlds whose 'European' or 'non-European' cultural character has been traditionally much debated. Moreover, there are no *a priori* theoretical or practical strictures which would prevent the postmodern cultural and political condition from overflowing to other regions because modernity has 'taken' in this way, by being transplanted into social worlds which could not generate it endogenously. The spread of modernity is for its part the seed-bed for the emergence of the postmodern cultural and political conditions in regions far beyond the cultural-geographical confines of 'Europe'. This is the precise circumstance which demands that *The Postmodern Political Condition* conclude with a critical inquiry into the 'European project'.

2

On Being Satisfied in a Dissatisfied Society I

The term 'dissatisfied society' has been coined in order to illuminate one conspicuous feature of western modernity. 'Dissatisfied society' is *not an essentialist* term. That is to say, it is not meant to designate the essence of modernity. Modernity can be described in accordance with many categories, each of which elicit one particular feature or other of the world epoch which differs from all those which have preceded it. The notion of a 'dissatisfied society' seeks to grasp the specificity of our world epoch from the perspective of *needs*, or, more particularly, from that of need-creation, need-perception, need-distribution and need-satisfaction. It suggests that the modern form of need-creation, need-perception and need-distribution reinforces dissatisfaction irrespective of whether or not any concrete need is actually satisfied. Furthermore, it suggests that a general dissatisfaction operates as a strong motivational force in the reproduction of modern societies. From this it would follow that if people cease to be dissatisfied with their lot – with their material wealth, their social position, their personal relationships, their knowledge and their performance on the one hand, and with their institutions, their social and political arrangements and the general state of affairs in the world on the other – modern society could no longer reproduce itself. At the very least, it would certainly enter an era of decay or decomposition, and would, no doubt, eventually collapse.

Even if then dissatisfaction is not 'the single essence' of modern society, it is certainly necessary to it. To look at modernity from the point of needs has two great advantages. Firstly, it allows us to view modernity in a *holistic* manner without this becoming a totalizing perspective. It is holistic in so far as one can assert that dissatisfaction keeps *all* institutions going and that it is inherent in each of them. But it will be non-totalizing for one certainly can also assert that no single modern institution or social or political arrangement is, by necessity, interlocked with all others. One can even assert, as we do, that there are three distinct developmental logics in western modernity: industrialization, capitalism and democracy. Furthermore, one can assert that the three logics can, and in fact do, contradict one another, that any of the three can subordinate the other two to itself to a greater or lesser extent. Thus understood, western modernity does not appear as a single 'totality'. Yet the advancement of each of the three logics requires the motivational force of dissatisfaction. Those committed to the logic of democracy, will be dissatisfied with the present state of affairs where the democratic logic is still to a great extent limited by, and subordinated to, the logic of industrialization and that of capitalism. Driven by this dissatisfaction, they will turn to others, equally dissatisfied with a fettered democracy, to urge them to press for a radicalization of democracy. Yet, since the holistic view is not a totalizing view, one may opt for change in one or another field of human interaction, but not in all of them. Put differently, one can mobilize one kind of dissatisfaction without mobilizing others.

The second advantage of viewing modernity from the perspective of needs presents itself in the possibility of combining two, distinct, discourses: the discourse of social philosophy and the discourse of existential philosophy. One can thematize the social creation, distribution, perception and satisfaction of needs, and one can equally thematize the individual's *subjective* relation to the system of needs, that is, the aspirations, enjoyments, sufferings and expectations of persons *qua* persons, their attachments to one another, their vulnerabilities, their cravings, their happiness and unhappiness. An earlier study, 'The dissatisfied society'[1] concentrated almost exclusively on the objective aspects of modern dissatisfaction. In what follows, we should like to examine the phenomenon of dissatisfaction from both sides, as it were, and thus shall combine the approaches of social philosophy and existential philosophy.

I

Each and every person is thrown into a particular world by the accident of birth. Nothing in our biological constitution or genetic endowments pre-determine that we should be born into one particular age rather than another, into one particular society rather than another, or into one particular social stratum rather than another. This is a generalized statement in that it refers to something which is the case always and everywhere: the *initial* contingency as the general condition of human existence. Denizens of the premodern world mobilized vast ideological resources to shield the social arrangements of domination and hierarchy against the awareness of contingency. Aristotle taught that slaves are born, not made, Brahmanism explained away contingency by the theory of reincarnation, and Christianity by God's will which allocates persons to their appropriate places in this vale of tears. Despite these and many other attempts to denying contingency, the awareness of initial contingency kept reappearing, especially amongst those born into the lower end of the social hierarchy. 'Had I been born an X, not a Y, what I could have achieved!' – such and similar statements were surely uttered many times in premodern societies by individuals of sensitivity and reflexivity. Yet the awareness of initial contingency was accompanied by the consciousness of *fate* in premodern societies. 'Since I was born a Y, I shall *not* achieve all that I could, had I been born an X.' The accident of birth determined one's place in the social division of labour. The frameworks of the way of life one could conduct were simply given and, as such, were truly pre-ordained. It was social arrangements that transformed contingency into necessity. Being born into the highest stratum meant being born with the optimal possibility of distinction. But these optimal possibilities too were pre-ordained and, as such, limited. Irrespective of whether fate decreed good fortune or bad, fate and contingency invariably merged into one.

In modern times a division of labour according to function was substituted for a stratified social division of labour. It was in this process that the general awareness of contingency emerged. Since the initial contingency of existence is no longer a *fate* of a kind that determines our ways of life, that denotes the boundaries of our actions and marks the limits of our possibilities, even though it may still be a hindrance or an asset, initial contingency itself becomes overdetermined. What had once been a fate, now becomes a context. Napoleon's famous dictum that every soldier carries the marshall's baton in his knapsack, expresses this altered situation and new awareness well. For if the accident of birth throws people into a context, instead of saddling them with the burden of fate, then neither the forms of life available, nor possibilities, are determined by birth. The individual himself or herself becomes the bearer of possibilities or, to put it in a more extreme form, the individual becomes tantamount to his/her as yet undefined and undetermined possibilities. Everything becomes possible. The total indeterminateness of the person, the absence of fate, and the transformation of the position at birth into a 'context' are the conditions of *secondary contingency*. It is not only being 'here' or 'there' that is conceived as contingent, so too is *the individual's relation* to a particular place and time as a mere 'context'. What a person makes of himself or herself, now depends on the person, even if not on the person alone. The person is the maker of his/her life, and in this sense is a *self-made man* or a *self-made woman*. Destiny, not fate, now defines the individual's relation to the world. Where fate determines possibilities, destiny lingers among possibilities, it has to be *caught*.

Yet it is not only the individual's relation to his/her initial 'context' that becomes contingent; the context itself also becomes contingent. Put simply, from a modern point of view, particular social arrangements and institutions can just as well exist as *not* exist. The world into which people are born is no longer seen as having been decreed by fate but as an agglomerate of possibilities. One can shape the world as much as one can shape oneself. At least in our imaginations, there are no limits to the possibilities for our 'shaping the world'. We can take the destiny of the world into our own hands. Just as our future depends on us, so too does the future of the world. How we can transform possibilities into destinies is now the question.

It was the idea of freedom that informed the awareness of contingency, and this was detected by all outstanding thinkers of the post-French-Revolutionary age. Marx emphasized that the workers' relation to their class is a contingent one. He had no doubt in his mind that the modern individual, the contingent person, the creator of his/her own destiny is a far superior being than the 'narrow-minded' individual of the premodern epoch. For Kierkegaard, *human existence* is defined by the category of possibility. Yet nineteenth-century thinkers did not hail contingency as an 'end in itself'. In their view, the freedom of mere possibility had to be transformed into freedom as destiny; freedom had to be merged with necessity, or at least it had to 'recognize' necessity or act upon it in order for it to be 'realized'. Both in its Hegelian and Marxian versions, the philosophy of history was invoked in order to sublate the contradiction between contingency and necessity. The traditional notion of fate was thus readmitted, as it were, through the back door. The worker has a contingent relation to

his class, and the very existence of the working class is itself
contingent, and yet the working class is the very class that recognizes
historical necessity, acts upon it and will establish a communist society
in accordance with the laws of history, that is: with necessity. This is
how the Marxian argument runs. Marx thus combined the awareness
of personal and historical contingency with the mediation of the
category of necessity. On the other pole, Kierkegaard succeeded in
eliminating fate completely in both its ancient and its streamlined,
modern, version. But in doing so he paid a heavy price: he regarded the
modern world as a context which can never be transformed into a
chosen destiny.

In the second half of the twentieth century, the concept of fate –
both the ancient and the more streamlined version – has been cast aside
for good. Consequently, we are now far more aware of our contingency
than ever before. Much contemporary philosophy expresses this
mental state very clearly. For instance, Sartre's thesis is that we are
thrown into freedom. Another philosopher, Unger, has argued
recently that we can just as easily imagine *not to be* as *to be*. Does it
make any difference for the world, or for others, that we exist rather
than not? Structuralists have even argued strenuously for the
elimination of the subject. The awareness of contingency, if not
attached to a consciousness of *destiny*, is frightening, and this is
precisely why we seek to eliminate it. To achieve this, people sometimes
jump headlong into movements which promise participation in
creating destiny. In this vein, Fromm explained the mass influence of
totalitarianism in Europe in terms of an 'escape from freedom'. Others
seek personal salvation in love: it is the Other, a single person who
becomes their destiny. Most people, however, fight the spectre of
contingency by becoming busy day and night or by amassing more and
more wealth or more and more power. Becoming 'somebody' seems to
be the royal road to overcoming contingency. But then, the 'mid-life
crisis' may set in and the person despairs. Contingency thus lurks
behind success.

According to an ancient Greek aphorism, no one can be called happy
before his death. What is different today however, is that people
cannot be called happy (in the sense of being satiated with life) on their
dying day either. Life's limitedness, the fate no human can overcome,
has become a fixed idea for modern humanity. Death has always been a
frightening horizon, but it has never been an *idée fixe* like it is now.
We are afraid of seeing a person die or of looking at the sight of death.
Since our common fate itself has become contingent, we are afraid of

looking it in its face. Suicide has become yet another gesture aimed at overcoming contingency: the contingency of death has been translated back in the terms of fate.

The existential question of modern life can be summed up as follows: how can we transform our contingency into our destiny without resigning freedom, without holding on to the banister of necessity or fate? How can we translate the social context into our own context without relapsing into experiments which have proved futile or fatal, into the experiments of social engineering or of redemptive politics?

II

The dissatisfied society is thus a society in which both social arrangements and persons become contingent. In a dissatisfied society all social and political arrangements can just as easily exist as not exist, they can be of one form or another. Similarly, the individual person can exist in it as well as not exist, and can play one role as much as another. Yet, even though all social arrangements could be different to what they are, the decisive social arrangements *may remain* unchanged (though not from any necessity) during the individual's formative years or, at least, undergo only slow changes. Although every person is the bearer of unlimited possibilities, having chosen a path in life, the individual person begins to confront diminishing possibilities and ever decreasing chances for a new beginning. Moreover, the *context* can become a hindrance to persons choosing a path of their liking and certain possibilities will never even occur to those who have chosen a particular path in life. As the German philosopher Koselleck put it, there is an enormous gap between expectations and experience. Expectations are imbued with contingency, yet what we experience are the hard facts of life, the factual limitation of our possibilities. The fateful and unbridgeable discrepancy between expectation and experience is a source of constant dissatisfaction and discontent.

The satisfaction in the present generation of certain needs that had remained dissatisfied in an earlier one will not make dissatisfaction decrease or abate. Since expectations constantly increase, the gap between expectation and experience remains as wide as it was to earlier generations; indeed, it can even widen. This is, as a rule, a source of embarrassment for the members of earlier generations. Parents frequently lecture their children by comparing their own lot to that of their offspring. 'When I was your age I wanted to go to college but my parents could not afford to send me. You attend a college – what more do you want?' Or: 'When I was your age, having an illegitimate child would bring great shame so that I would sooner have had an abortion than give birth to the child I so dearly wanted. But today you can have your child, and even some financial support to bring it up – what more could you want?' Children, as a rule, answer such attitudes in the following terms: 'I am sorry but we are living in different times. What would have been good enough for you, is not good enough for us. We need something more.' And the parents' standard rebuke: 'You are too spoilt', is the wrong answer. For higher expectations change both the quality and the quantity of needs, and the children measure their experience with their *own* expectations, and not with those of their parents.

What children claim in their dialogue with the members of a previous generation is *the recognition of their needs*. The parents' dictum that the cause of the children's dissatisfaction is their being spoilt is tantamount to withholding recognition of such needs. They *explain* the accusation of 'being spoilt' by assuming that *all their children's needs have been met*. The explanation itself suggests that the children's needs are regarded as *irrational*. What underlies this attitude is, of course, the parents' self-identification with their children whom they regard as their own replicas, the only difference being that the former generation sees in the expanded need-satisfaction of their offspring, which still leaves the latter dissatisfied, the actualization of their boldest aspirations, and the parents therefore regard their children's dissatisfaction as irrational. Moreover, this is not a one-way street: when the children remain dissatisfied, the supreme need of the parents is not met. Often, even the *recognition* of the parents' needs is withheld for they are so 'narrow-minded' and 'conservative', their ideas so 'wrong and outdated'. In this case, it is the child who asserts the *irrationality* of the parents' needs.

Our discussion thus far leads us to raise the following set of interrelated questions: can needs be rational and irrational? Is it legitimate to make the following distinctions: this particular group of people has good reason for its dissatisfaction, whereas that particular group of people has no reason at all for being dissatisfied? Or, this particular person has good reason for being dissatisfied, while that particular person has none at all? Or, is the following distinction legitimate: this particular group of people (or this particular person) has all the reasons in the world to be dissatisfied, and yet they are satisfied? Should we come to the conclusion that certain needs are rational whereas others are not, would such a distinction entitle us to *withhold* recognition from the non-rational ones? Finally, can people be *enjoined* to have or not to have certain needs? That is, is it legitimate for us to say to someone: 'you are satisfied although you *ought to be* dissatisfied?

Needs can be described as conscious feelings of '*something lacking*'. As a result, the term 'need' does not denote one particular concrete feeling but many distinct feeling in their quality of *signaling a lack*. Not all feelings can signal a 'lack' but many as different as hunger, curiosity, anxiety, love and countless others certainly do. Most needs are composite feelings, so-called 'feeling dispositions'. The conscious feeling of a lack of something is also a motivation: the lack has to be filled, eliminated. The filling, or the elimination, of the lack implies the preservation or the *expansion* of the Self. Or, to formulate it the other way round: without the feeling of something lacking, the Self cannot be preserved or, even less, expanded. The feeling of something lacking itself is not equivalent to dissatisfaction. Dissatisfaction can only be asserted if the feeling that something is lacking is perpetuated or if it is intensifying. This happens if (a) the means for the satisfaction of needs (satisfiers) which are *socially ascribed* to a person or a group of persons are not available to the particular person or group of persons, (b) if satisfiers which are in principle within the reach of the person, albeit not socially ascribed to him or her, inform the person, create the need in the person and yet they are not (cannot be) acquired by the person, and (c) if the lack cannot be filled, or eliminated by *any* satisfier or if the person feels the lack *without knowing* what it is that he/she needs.

In the first case, in the absence of socially ascribed satisfiers, we normally tend to regard both needs and dissatisfaction (in so far as needs are not met) *as rational*. Our usual comment on such a situation runs as follows: these people have every reason for being dissatisfied. What kinds of needs are regarded as rational and for whom, depends then on *social ascription*, on social norms and values. Aspirations, social norms and values, standards of need-satisfaction like this change within one society and they vary from society to society, from culture to culture. In modern society, standards of need-satisfaction, as a rule, undergo fairly rapid changes; sometimes we have two or more sets of standards instead of one. And yet there are cases of need-ascription which are almost consensual. We have no hesitation in stating that the unemployed have every reason for being dissatisfied because we, almost consensually, regard unemployment as an anomaly, and we agree that the need for finding employment is one which should be met. Similarly, if a woman today is kept in tutelage by her husband, we would agree that she has every reason for being dissatisfied with her marriage, although half a century ago most people would have disagreed.

In the third case, when a particular need cannot be met with any available satisfiers or when the person feels that there is something lacking without knowing what the lack consists of, and therefore without having the faintest idea about the kinds of satisfier that may meet his/or her need, we normally regard the needs in question as *irrational*. For a disbeliever, the need for immortality is irrational. All needs which pertain to the awareness of our common initial contingency are irrational by definition (like the need for being born rich when one was born poor, the need for being born a man when one was born a woman, the need for being born with musical talents when one is born tone deaf, and so on). The awareness of initial contingency can be accompanied by steady dissatisfaction. Yet since the need to be someone else, or somewhere else, cannot by definition be met, the dissatisfaction ensuing therefrom is regarded as irrational. Anxieties and neuroses can also indicate dissatisfaction. Yet as long as we are unable to understand and explain them, as long as we continue to be unaware of what is being missed, what is lacking in our life, such and similar feelings of discontent are also irrational.

From our point of view, the most interesting grounds for dissatisfaction is (b) for it is precisely the needs which appear in this cluster that keep the dissatisfied society going. In principle, all avenues of life are open to each and every person. In principle, each and every person is free to acquire wealth fame or power, and if they acquire some, they can acquire more. In principle, each and every person can acquire such kinds of excellence as are rewarded by a far higher degree of social recognition than others. In principle, each and every person can achieve all these, though in fact only few do. Needs are, or can be, informed by possible satisfiers but the actual satisfaction of such needs will be within the reach of a few only. This is the situation which has been described as the abyss between expectations and life experiences. Yet it would be overly one-sided to refer only to aspirations grounded in the images of social power, of wealth or fame, that is to say, in the kind of needs which, in English, are typically termed 'wants'. The universal values of freedom and life are universal and general precisely because they can inform all kinds of aspirations related to all types and forms of human interactions, institutions, forms of life which are defined as 'goods', as 'valuable'. Human relations based on equality and on the free and mutual recognition of persons are such goods; they are valuable, no matter whether they refer to relations between genders, friends, associates or citizens. Needs for goods of intrinsic worth are not wants, they cannot be met by wealth, by position or by fame, and their satisfaction excludes the use of power against other human beings. All such aspirations are comprised in, though they are not reducible to, the value of *self-determination*.

Both the needs which are simultaneously wants and the needs which are not wants, have something to do with the *secondary contingency* of social life. The contingent person, who feels that he/she could just as well exist as not exist, seeks to shed this contingency as we have already mentioned, becoming 'somebody' presents itself as an avenue for transforming contingency into destiny. To seek self-determination offers itself as yet another avenue. The two aspirations can also be combined. Feminist movements have aimed at opening the first avenue for women, but now they are more concerned with the second. We will return to this question shortly.

The dissatisfied society is characterized by the *expansion* of both wants and needs. We have seen that needs are feelings and, simultaneously, motivational forces. In modern times, such motivational forces appear as *claims* both in the social and and the political arena. People in need make a *claim* for the satisfaction of their needs. In making such claims, people translate their *personal* dissatisfactions into a public language, into that of justice and equity. Having translated these needs into the language of justice and equity, actors make a plea for the substitution of new social and political rules and laws for existing ones so that the gap between aspirations and experiences might be bridged. Should new rules and laws be successfully implemented, new claims will also make their appearance. Needs belonging to cluster (b) comprise the motivational forces of progress. The efficacy of this drive for progress is dependent upon the quality and quantity of satisfiers which are, in principle, if not in reality, available to all. If the quality of satisfiers is constant, the drive for progress implies an ever greater quantity of certain satisfiers, or a more equitable distribution of 'available satisfiers'. Needs as wants and needs for self-determination which are not wants, are qualitatively different. One might lay claims for an increasing quantity of the first, from the second or for both. At the present stage of western modernity, social imaginations are preoccupied with wants rather than with needs which are other than wants. Progress here is defined as an increase in wants, or, more correctly, as an increase in the satisfiers of wants. Yet the two kinds of claims might, at least to a degree, also be combined if the claim for more satisfiers of wants is made jointly with the claim for a more equitable distribution or availability of satisfiers. But even where such a combination is effected, it is claims which centre on the satisfiers of wants which are predominant. The fact that progress is generally gauged by indicators such as per capita production illustrates well the predominance of wants and the satisfiers of wants in our social imagination.

All needs formulated as claims are *rational*. The very fact that they are formulated as claims makes them rational. To formulate a claim means that one gives *reasons* as to why a particular need ought to be met, even though it is not. Claims make a case for the social ascription of satisfiers which are not as yet socially ascribed. A person whose needs are not met can be said to be *rationally* dissatisfied whenever his/her needs can be related to claims and thus justified by claims. However, in complex societies there are many claims for certain satisfiers and claims may contradict one another. They contradict one another if the needs awaiting satisfaction cannot simultaneously be satisfied, if the satisfaction of one need requires the prolongation of dissatisfaction in respect to another need. In such cases, those who make a claim for the satisfaction of needs in cluster (a) will declare needs belonging in cluster (b) to be irrational and vice versa. A particular kind of dissatisfaction which to the advocates of needs in cluster (a) appears rational, will be regarded as irrational by those advocating the satisfaction of needs in cluster (b). But how are we to decide which are *really* rational if both parties can give reasons for the priority of their respective clusters of needs? Is there an objective measure with which to decide upon the rationality or irrationality of such needs? For the moment let us assume that both kinds of dissatisfaction are rational even though both claims may not be of equal weight.

But what if a person can formulate and justify a need, and any decision ensuing therefrom, without having to thematize them as claims? To be sure, claims in themselves presuppose that certain needs are publicly recognized by some. But what happens if a private claim unveils a need which is publicly recognized by *no one*? Needs sometimes make their first appearance in gestures of disobedience and rebellion. A disobedient or rebellious person may not be able to justify his/her needs, generalize them, or make a claim for their satisfaction; it may well be that such a person might only be capable of expressing them. If needs are *merely made manifest* by gestures (through words and actions and without reasons being given to justify them), they are not yet rational. But the same needs can become rational if they become widespread and can be justified by values as well as translated into the language of claims. Not all irrational needs however, become rational, indeed not all of them *can* become rational. But the fact that new needs sometimes appear as irrational is sufficient reason for us to conclude that all needs should be recognized *as real*, and not just rational ones. Yet the recognition of the reality of needs does not imply a recognition of their legitimacy. A need can only be recognized as legitimate if its satisfaction does not include the use of another person as a mere means. Let us refer back to our earlier example of generational conflicts. The parents' recognition of the rational needs of the child, that is, of those needs which have been formulated as public claims, is obviously warranted, though this should not mean that they have thereby relinquished their right to be critical of those needs. Moreover, even the parents' recognition of the non-rational needs of the child may be warranted as would any support they might give the child in aiding him or her in translating such needs into a language of claims. Yet the parents should certainly not recognize as legitimate those needs which can only be satisfied by using other people (be it the child's siblings, parents or friends) as mere means, by exploiting and dominating them.

The rigid division between value-rationality and goal-rationality is particularly irrelevant if applied to needs. In the case of irrational needs both values and purposes can be equally obscure. If, for example, dissatisfaction appears as a state of indeterminate discontent, the person does not even know *why* he or she 'does not find his/her place' or why he or she is in a state of constant anxiety. The first requirement in making a claim for the legitimacy of a need is to be aware of the source of dissatisfaction. Making a need-claim is the procedure by which a certain kind of need is related to a certain kind of value. If we cannot make a claim, we fall short of value-rationality. At the same time, irrational needs do not motivate us towards the attainment of certain goals either. Rational needs, on the contrary, appear as value-claims and they simultaneously motivate us in the achievement of certain goals or in the undertaking of certain actions which are considered to be ends in themselves.

III

We have distinguished two types of needs which keep our dissatisfied society moving: wants, on the one hand and needs for self-determination on the other. We have, thus far, made no evaluative distinction between these two kinds of needs. There were times when wants were, at least within leftist discourse, totally devalued. It was assumed that we already had an abundance of satisfiers, that we were living in an 'affluent society' and therefore that our wants were irrational, imaginary or unreal. We hardly need remind ourselves today of the slums of western cities, and the dire poverty and hopelessness of those dwelling in them to realize how wrong we all were. Not even in well-established welfare states such as Sweden or Austria, could one unequivocally assert the existence of a reign of generalized affluence. Yet even if we assume that the 'elementary needs' of all are indeed met, new wants continue to be produced daily, and if people feel such needs and make claims for their satisfaction, no one has the right to ascribe their needs to false consciousness, to arbitrariness, or to mere fancy. To be more precise: no particular concrete want invested in a particular concrete satisfier, or even in a great number of such concrete satisfiers, can legitimately be devalued and rejected as unreal or false. Rather than devaluing any concrete want in any concrete satisfier, whatever its nature, let us compare the clusters of satisfiers which correspond to needs and wants.

As mentioned, within modernity there has emerged a strong awareness of contingency and this has been accompanied by serious efforts to eliminate contingency by transforming it into destiny. Contingency is a state of indeterminate possibilities. Indeterminate possibilities are freedom and life-chances in their abstractness for they are simultaneously everything and nothing. The merely contingent person is nothing for he/she has not as yet actualized any of his/her possibilities, but he/she is also everything for he/she has not yet excluded any possibility from being actualized.

In living our lives in one way or another, in making choices, in opting for one or another profession, in being dedicated to one thing rather than to another, in living with one particular person rather than with another, we exclude certain possibilities from actualization whilst actualizing others. When we realize that we might have made other choices, that we might have actualized other possibilities than the ones we have, we rightly regard ourselves as trapped in a state of contingency with reduced life-chances and reduced freedom. On the other hand, if we realize that we could not possibly have chosen any other path in life than the one we did, and that we have actualized the *very possibilities* which were the best of all our endowments, we are no longer contingent. In such circumstances, we should certainly have transformed our life from contingency into destiny. When Luther said: 'here I stand and cannot do otherwise', his was a statement of destiny which left no residues of contingency remaining. One need not be a Luther to reach this stage. A considerable proportion of the members of any human community would simply not entertain the idea that they might have chosen possibilities other than the ones they actually chose. These people know that they leave a trace on the very world they dwell in by virtue of *being what they are and doing what they do*; that is, they know that their existence makes a difference.

To be satisfied in a dissatisfied society has nothing to do with the satisfaction of all concrete needs. If all concrete needs could possibly be met, we would no longer be living in a dissatisfied society. It is Weber's profound observation that we, unlike our forebears, cannot die 'satiated with life'. We cannot be satiated with the state of the world, we cannot come to know everything we have wanted to know, we cannot see everything we have wanted to see, we cannot do everything we have wanted to do, in short, we cannot achieve everything we have wanted to achieve. But we can achieve the transformation of our contingency into destiny. If someone succeeds in transforming his/her contingency into his/her destiny, if someone can reiterate Luther's words: 'here I stand and I cannot do otherwise', if someone is aware that his/her existence makes a difference, that he/she leaves a trace on the face of the world, such a person will be satisfied with his/her life as a whole and can say that he/she has become what, in the light of available possibilities, he/she was able to become. Rosa Luxemburg's calm words from prison when she was coming ever closer to her violent death: *ultra posse, nemo obligatur*, convey precisely this meaning. She was satisfied with her life even though she had absolutely no reason to be satisfied with the state of world she was about to leave or, for that matter, with her own personal fate. Yet it is not fate but destiny that makes up for our contingency.

It should by now be clear from our discussion thus far that it is the satisfaction of the needs for self-determination, and not that of mere wants that best allows the transformation of our contingency into destiny. The satisfaction of wants is seen as the avenue for transforming contingency into destiny because want-satisfaction carries the promise of increase in self-determination. If one is destitute, powerless and unknown, self-determination is indeed a remote possibility. It is not mere 'false consciousness' that makes people believe that acquiring more and more things and ever greater power or fame is the royal road to self-determination. And it would be utterly foolish, indeed conceited, to deny that having something, having a certain power or enjoying a measure of fame can contribute to self-determination. Yet if people are orientated towards the satisfaction of wants alone and they expect self-determination to emerge as the end result of want-satisfaction, the end result will not materialize or at least not materialize fully. The reason for this is that all wants are determined *from the outside* and *not from inside*. Technology, social circumstances, political institutions determine and provide a plethora of satisfiers for such wants. A want-orientated person seeks self-determination in subjecting himself or herself to a kind of determination which does not stem from the Self's own choice. Moreover, if a Self is intent on satisfying his/her wants alone, then the satisfaction of wants may run counter to the satisfaction of the wants of others. This is the case in particular if need-satisfaction is orientated to gaining more and more power. Apart from the justified social and political criticism of a need satisfaction of this kind, any person who gains self-determination at the expense of others can never be secure. The moment such a person loses wealth, power of fame, he/she will be thrown back to a state of mere contingency. For this reason, it is more promising to seek self-determination directly, not indirectly; that is to say, to seek a kind of self-determination which is not achieved at the expense of others, which does not require being totally determined by satisfiers provided by circumstances or powers external to the self. One can seek self-determination directly in one of two distinct ways. Firstly, one can concentrate on the development of one's own abilities or, secondly, one can project the self-determination of others simultaneously with one's own. Not self-deification, but self-abandonment to tasks and causes, not self-centredness, but a readiness for co-operation with our fellow-creatures, is what distinguishes the second road to self-determination. Whenever we refer to seeking self-determinating in a direct way, we always have the second option in mind.

Seeking self-determination directly and indirectly are *two distinct attitudes* both of which we can equally adopt in modern life. Yet even the first attitude does not exclude a striving for want-satisfaction, nor does it exclude external determination. Self-determination does not require, nor does it even permit, the absolute freedom of total and complete autonomy. One can, of course, adopt the lifestyle of a hermit in the desert though such courses are hardly generalizable. If they were, our society would cease to be a 'dissatisfied' one, indeed it would cease to exist. Such individualistic fantasies are neither real nor desirable options.

We are thrown by the accident of birth into the present, into our world, into the dissatisfied society. The world has become a 'context', the context for our indeterminate possibilities. Self-determination is not context-free; indeed coping with its context is its intrinsic feature.

The question implied in the title of this chapter is the following: how can one be satisfied in a dissatisfied society? From the argument thus far, we have concluded that we can be satisfied with our lives even if we cannot satisfy all our needs, provided that we succeed in transforming our contingency into self-determination. The optimal course for the transformation of our contingency into self-determination is seeking self-determination directly, without renouncing the satisfaction of our wants. Yet this attitude requires coping with our context. Our context need not be determined by us in order for us to achieve self-determination. We need not recognize necessity of any kind in our context, we need not understand ourselves as caretakers of such a necessity in order to achieve self-determination. Yet we have to act upon our context. For only if we have done so can we say with Rosa Luxemburg: *ultra posse, nemo obligatur*. But *how* can we cope with our context in such a way?

Note

A. Heller, *The Power of Shame. A rational perspective* (Routledge and Kegan Paul, London, 1984).

3

On Being Satisfied in a Dissatisfied Society II

The dissatisfied society is continually changing. These changes can be attributed to the expanded self-reproduction of a self-propelling system, as well as the interventions and actions of subjects, both individual and collective. The two approaches can also be combined. We do not have any *single* objective description of modern society. All descriptions, however scientific, are embedded in, and informed by, evaluative and philosophical theories and meta-theories. Although we have not sought here to define the structure of modern society, it should be clear that we attribute the power of intervention, of bringing about changes, to (single or collective) subjects. We adopt the position, and the *regard*, of the contingent person who is intent on transforming his/her contingency into a destiny, not through the satisfaction of mere wants, not even by detaching himself or herself from a context but by coping with the context while giving priority to the satisfaction of the needs of self-determination. Coping with a context means changing it, giving priority to the satisfaction of the needs of self-determination means changing that context, to the extent possible, in a direction which allows greater self-determination. A position such as the one we have outlined does not stand in great favour in contemporary social theory. The latest trend within social theory, which is termed post-structuralist or postmodernist, theorizes contingency not only as a historical product but also as a permanent feature of human life. In becoming contingent, the subject disappears. Endeavouring to transform contingency into destiny is regarded as erroneous, the illusory belief of a humanistic discourse which has to be abandoned. Viewed from this perspective, a social structure will appear either as a negative totality or as a fragmented text that we cannot read, a force-field of micro-power-relationships, an iron cage of self-reproducing necessity, alienated, thing-like, reified. If we adopt an alternative image of the subject – for example, as the repository of communicative competence, as Habermas does, or as the fountainhead of an alternative imaginary as Castoriadis does – the world will appear in a different light. At the very least, this will enable us to provide an additional account of human contingency based upon very different sets of categories.

In one of his most recent studies, Habermas has pointed to the increasing intransparency (*Undurchsichtigkeit*) of the modern world.[1] No society is completely transparent, yet some are more transparent than others. Totalitarian societies have a great degree of transparency because they are organized around a single centre. Anyone who lives in such a society knows that the operation of all branches and sub-systems of the society are dependent on this single centre. Traditional societies were also more transparent, for similar reasons. If social actors are intent on changing a relatively transparent society, they know precisely what needs to be done even if they cannot do it. In both types of societies, an immobilizing of the centre will effectively arrest the reproduction of the social systems. The modern western state, however, has no organizing centre: as Luhmann puts it, the social system has become de-centred. In Luhmann's view, modern society consists of a great variety of systems, and each and every system serves as the environment for all others which they surround or by which they are surrounded. One can subscribe to such a view of modern societies without thereby being committed to a systems theory. To such a view, we would add only that the three developmental logics of western modernity (capitalism, industrialization and democracy) are embedded in those systems, though not in all of them and not even to an equal extent in each one.

Certain systems which operate in modern welfare states are sub-systems of the world-system (in the main, these are economic ones), others are sub-systems of a territorial or cultural system (such as alliances, international institutions), others again are the systems of a single state (such as the welfare system). This general differentiation is one reason for our dispensing with the idea that the modern western social system is organized around any one single centre. Another reason concerns the status of everyday life. At this point we also depart from Luhmann's systems theory because, in our view, everyday life cannot be seen as a system. Each person is brought up in an everyday context where the person learns to use ordinary language, *man-made* objects and acquires a certain background knowledge comprising facts and values, as well as a readiness to observe norms and rules. Although systems encroach upon everyday life, although scientific discourse exerts an enormous influence on our ideas of the good life, although life-worlds (that is, the sum total of shared cultural and normative patterns) become pluralistic and diffuse, everyday life still stands out as a separate sphere. The conflicts occurring in this sphere belong to our *basic life experiences* and they may develop needs in us for which we are ready to make claims. Cultural and normative patterns are not absorbed by systems or the institutional spheres (understood as the combination of several interconnected systems). This is obvious if we consider that there exists a *loose ethos*, a background ethos in society which informs practices within all spheres and systems. These factors underscore our contention that our world becomes increasingly opaque, though we would hasten to add the qualification that in a small body politic, opacity is not as prevalent as it is within large states. If viewed in such terms then, small states, all other conditions being equal, stand a better chance for conscious human intervention than large ones, even if they are equally de-centred.

If this approach is correct, modern western welfare society cannot be described as a *totality*, be it positive or negative. It is simply *not* a totality. And since it is not, it cannot be changed as a totality either. The traditional anarchist view, according to which only the state needs to be abolished and everything will be changed for the better, into a society without force, domination and hierarchy, is completely outdated. The same must be said for the orthodox Marxist view according to which the state apparatuses have to be seized and destroyed, the rule of the working class established, the market abolished, so that a completely new and egalitarian society will come into being. These and similar projects constitute instances of *redemptive politics*.[3] A redemptive politics is one in which a single final gesture is seen as the carrier of ultimate redemption both for society and each and every person dwelling within it. The more de-centred a social system becomes, the more simple-minded redemptive politics appears (and we can disregard here the dangers inherent in the redemptive paradigm). It is this loss of relevance suffered by the redemptive paradigm that has led so many to despair. The theory of 'negative dialectics' is the offspring of precisely this kind of despair. Such despair, however, is misplaced, for if there is no social redemption, neither is there damnation.

The absence of any single organizing centre in modern western societies does not decrease the possibility for action, nor the capacity for changing social relationships. Action potentials are simply relocated. Precisely because of the de-centred character of the social system, emancipatory actions need not focus on changing a single, all-encompassing and dominating centre or institution but they can be pursued in every system and sub-system, in all spheres of society including everyday life. In this context, emancipatory action becomes diffuse. Moreover, it is no longer necessary for *all* actors who aim at emancipation to join forces, as such a 'joining of forces' was necessary only as long as one could pinpoint a single organizing centre of all social sub-systems. Different groups of actors can engage in emancipatory action within different systems and spheres (including everyday life). Modern society does not resemble a building which must be pulled down before a new one can be erected. If we must use similes at all, it resembles more closely a ship on which one group can change the masts, the other can change the sails, while a third can be busy with refurbishing the deck. Of course, similes can be misleading. If one changes one particular sub-system, one immediately influences the environment of that sub-system. If everyday life has been changed here and there, if cultural sub-spheres have been changed to a degree, the society itself will have been changed even if the changes were implemented by different groups of actors without any uniting of forces. The model of modern society which we have sketched here allows us to see how we might transform our contingency into our destiny while coping with our context. People have different needs, as well as distinct structures of needs, and it is highly unlikely that the same patterns of action will suit each and every one. It is equally unlikely that the same types of practices will bridge the gap between their experiences and expectations given the individual and idiosyncratic character of both.

We have already mentioned briefly our conception of modernity as a constellation of three distinct, though interrelated logics.[4] Even the briefest consideration of the logics of industrialization would show that the motivational forces which perpetuate each of these logics are *wants*. Industrialization and capitalism provide satisfiers for wants. In doing so they may also provide satisfiers for self-determination, though without thereby satisfying the need for self-determination as such. It is the logic of democracy alone which can be upheld and expanded by those needs which aim at self-determination. An institution is fully democratic if all the norms and rules of that particular institution have been devised and authorized by the free will of every member who is party to that institution. Yet it is not the condition of democracy that the *function* (or functions) of a particular institution should also be decided or co-determined by its members: certain institutions *must* perform certain functions and not others. One might, for instance, make a case for self-management within factories but this does not mean that the question whether or not factories should produce certain material goods itself becomes a matter of decision. Religious institutions are institutions of worship and the disseminators of particular faiths. The members of such institutions cannot therefore freely decide to practise computer technology instead. Eliminating basic functions can only mean eliminating the institution itself, not its democratization.

Certain conclusions can be drawn from these considerations:

1   It makes sense to aim at increasing self-determination in any sub-system and sphere, including everyday life, irrespective of whether or not the same process has been triggered in other spheres or systems.

2   It makes sense equally to trigger such a process in any particular institution (no matter whether it is an institution of production, education, welfare, culture or political arbitration) irrespective of whether or not the same process has been triggered in other institutions of *the same* sub-system or *the same* sphere.

3   Further, it is possible to emphasize *one aspect* of self-determination irrespective of whether self-determination in other respects has been triggered or not.

4   An increase in self-determination (democratization) does not aim at the elimination of the functional division of labour (between sub-systems and spheres) characteristic of modernity. Yet if the pursuit for self-determination is successful, and to the extent that it is, transfunctional action can gather momentum both within particular institutions and at a cross-institutional level.

5   The logic of democracy, if furthered and advanced, can thus become the dominant logic of modernity asserting its primacy over the other two (those of capitalism and industrialization), though not eliminating them completely. Needs for self-determination do not reduce wants to a state of stagnation. Once needs for self-determination begin to be met on an increasing scale, one could rightly assume that this will result in a diffusion of wants in satisfiers of different quality and quantity rather than in a new brand of self-denial or asceticism.

The projected radicalization of democracy we have sketched here appears to be strongly Utopian. Yet so many institutions which we now take for granted were once Utopian, such that the association of Utopia with unfeasibility is completely unjustifiable.

Up to this point, we have sought to show that western modernity, as it now stands, does not exclude the possibility of an increase in self-determination. The fact that modern, western, societies have lost their organizing centres allows greater possibilities for a project of democratization than would otherwise be the case. Opacity in itself is not an obstacle to emancipatory action, as long as action itself is not devised as totalizing.

I have made mention of two kinds of processes of democratization: one which triggers such processes within an institution, a project, a cultural sphere and the like and another which triggers such processes from one aspect of life and does so cross-institutionally. Neither process is unheard of, and even less are they unimaginable, in contemporary societies. There are self-managed factories, offices, schools, agricultural communities, associations and the like. If a housing project is launched those who are to live in the houses could decide what kind of houses, flats and surroundings should be constructed: the tenants could make recommendations for such a use of allocated resources as best accommodates their needs and values. Such and similar practices, projects and movements comprise intra-institutional aims. Feminism, the single most important movement for self-determination, by contrast, is trans-institutional. It is obvious that feminism is a movement for self-determination. As Simone de Beauvoir pointed out at a time when the movement was still in a state of gestation, women's place in the world has always been determined by the *regard* of the male. If a person was thrown into the world as female, her fate was sealed. The consciousness of contingency could never develop in women as it did in men. A man could speak in such terms: 'had I been born a nobleman, I could have achieved this and that' and he could, no doubt, enumerate the highest types of achievement, the most subtle forms of distinction of his world. But a woman would always have to add to this: 'had I been born a man!' A man could place himself, that is, his own person into another *environment* whereas a woman was reduced to an *imaginary* change of her *biological constitution*, of her whole being, for it was precisely this constitution that determined her and limited her possibilities. The female existence determined by the male's *regard* was all-encompassing. The female was determined by this *regard* in her everyday life, in all spheres and systems, sub-systems and institutions. It was this all-encompassing determination that has been challenged by feminist movements. Women's movements prior to contemporary (second-wave) feminism had already challenged this determination within one or another sphere. They did so in the political sphere when they fought for universal suffrage and in the institutions of production when they fought for equal wages. But second-wave feminism has made this challenge all-encompassing. Women now fight for a dual contingency: for the indeterminateness of their possibilities and for the preconditions of self-determination. Normally, women who fight for the preconditions of their self-determination also develop a heightened sensitivity to all kinds of contestation which aim at increasing possibilities for self-determination

II

Let us now return to the main topic of this chapter: how can we be satisfied in a dissatisfied society? The broadest lines of the answer have already been drawn. We can be satisfied with our *lives* to the extent that we are able to transform our dual contingency into our destiny by choosing to satisfy our needs for self-determination directly and not indirectly. To be satisfied with our lives does not mean being generally satisfied. We can be dissatisfied with the state of the world, further we can be dissatisfied with not having achieved this or that, we can still be dissatisfied with people, with the limitations of our knowledge and so on. We can be certain in advance that several of our *concrete* needs will not be met. And yet we may remain satisfied with our lives as a whole, and greater, deeper satisfaction is not even warranted. Put another way, modern women and men do not possess the *need* to be completely satisfied. For if they were, this would mean the end of striving and seeking which is after all our life element. It would mean resigning from any further development. Those who are satisfied with their lives will not see themselves as mere means for a goal which is to be achieved in some distant future. Yet they do not regard themselves and their destiny as final ends either. Their life is *an end* precisely because it also has a *purpose beyond the individual's self-realization*.

If the end of the individual is self-determination, then the higher purpose to which the individual is committed is likely to be the self-determination of others. Put the other way round: aiming at the self-determination of others is the very purpose beyond the individual's self-realization which is never to the detriment of the person's self-determination. A person is a member of groups, institutions and party to personal relationships. In this capacity, he/she seeks the self-determination of all members of such groups, institutions and personal relationships, as well as his/her own self-determination in being committed to a value or a purpose that stands higher than the person. At this point, the following objection could be raised. It stands to reason, one might argue, that if a person succeeds in the project of self-determination within self-selected groups, institutions and relationships, then his/her own self-determination will indeed be achieved. But what if the person fails? What if, despite the person's dedication to such a purpose, self-determination is not increased within any of the groups of institutions the person is affiliated with? Since this happens frequently, the achievement of self-determination seems to be threatened. This would certainly be a valid counter-argument were our position a totalizing one, an option formulated in terms of an absolute 'either–or': either the whole of society must be changed in the direction of self-determination or else the purpose itself is defeated and no personal self-determination can be achieved. But we have rejected any totalizing approach. We believe that those who can state with conviction: 'if a second life were granted me, I would do exactly the same, I would like to become the same person I have become', have already achieved self-determination. And statements like this can be made even if our projects have failed. In addition, from the position of a de-totalizing view of social relationships it seems very unlikely that such projects will fail in every instance. We can succeed at least on one count: we can shape our personal relationships, for example friendships, as relationships of self-determination. If at least our intimate and friendly contacts are based on symmetric reciprocity, mutual respect and common cause and purpose, we have already created a social space of self-determination where our own self-determination and that of others presuppose one another. And it is certainly not excluded that, *together with others*, we can contribute to an increase in self-determination in broader-based human groups and institutions as well. 'Together with others' is the decisive qualification here. If a group of people in 'being together' seek to increase the possibilities for self-determination, the group itself must already have been based on the principle of self-determination.

Contingency can be transformed into destiny if 'coping with the context' at least includes a widening of the space of self-determination. 'Coping with the context' includes many, quite heterogeneous, activities. It would be ridiculous to assert that 'coping with the context' should be, or even could be, coextensive with opening a space for self-determination in concert with others. Understanding the world, passing judgements on actors, analysing, criticizing, accepting or rejecting social and political institutions and events outside the radius of the person's action, are also aspects of 'coping with the context'. So too is the choice of profession and professional activity itself, work, the satisfaction of wants and so much else. Yet if one is committed to a widening of the space for self-determination, this aspect of 'coping with the context' will colour, if not determine, all other modes of 'coping'. The project of self-determination works as a *tonic* in giving tone and vigour to everything else, not as a single cause.

There are at least two parties to the opening of any new space of self-determination. In a group or an institution, there are far more parties for every member of the group or institution is a party to it. Of course, the project of self-determination in a group or institution has to be *initiated* by someone. In an optimal case, the initiative would come from all parties concerned, though this would occur only in the most extreme circumstances. Normally however, it is only a few who take the initiative. Those who initiate have to consider seriously the following problem: *how* can a new space for self-determination be opened, and how might one proceed in opening it? The initiators of projects of self-determination will certainly confront countervailing tendencies and even immobilism though they must always resist the idea that people can be forced to be free. The idea of forcing people into freedom invariably serves as an ideological device for a new kind of domination. There is only one kind of sublime pressure which is difficult to avoid: the pressure of rhetoric. Rhetoric is an art of persuasion. It permits the use of all manner of verbal devices designed to lead another party to accept a proposition for action. It permits the manipulation of facts, the withholding of certain items of information and the overemphasizing of others, it appeals to non-rational emotions (envy, vanity, aggression) and the like. It has been the philosopher's habit to contrast rhetoric to dialectics. In this vein, a discussion is dialectical if all parties to the discussion stand in a symmetrically reciprocal relationship with one another, if everyone is a speaker at the same time as a listener and if all participants give reasons in support of their views. A dialectical relationship presupposes that all facts relevant to the decision are equally available to all parties and that appeal to merely particularistic emotions (including irrational ones) is unwarranted. By contrast, a discussion is rhetorical if participants to a discussion stand in an asymmetrical relationship. Thus, to return to the problem which concerns us here, if people initiate the opening of a new space for self-determination, they must endeavour not to proceed rhetorically. Whilst this is an objective which is not always easy to attain, it is a serious test of the authenticity of our intentions.

It must always be borne in mind that embarking on something new is always an *experiment*. Both here and elsewhere, we have made a case for the validity of the following regulative idea: all needs should be recognized, and recognized equally excepting those whose satisfaction implies the use of other persons as mere means. It follows from this that if a social experiment is undertaken, all parties to the experiment must be equally willing to undertake such an experiment. No one is entitled to experiment with others, we can only experiment together. Where the experiment is one which seeks self-determination there are *two elements* which should be distinguished. The first is the process of self-determination itself. The second concerns the *result* of the process of self-determination. We can all decide at any moment that the norms and rules of our group or a particular institution should be determined by all of us and that everyone should equally be party to such decisions. But we can also *set* particular rules and norms for ourselves as equal parties to the decision. The first element of the experiment may be successfully accomplished whilst the second may remain beyond reach. That is, we may be able to agree upon the procedural principles which ought to guide the particular experiment in self-determination but not on the content of the norms and rules themselves. How can the initiators of such a dual-faceted experiment proceed dialectically if all needs, except those which rely upon domination and the use of force, are recognized at once? They must distinguish between needs for self-determination on the one hand and all other needs and their corresponding satisfiers on the other. This sounds fairly straightforward although many decisive mistakes have been committed precisely because sufficient heed has not been paid to such a distinction. To use a well-known example, Simone de Beauvoir made a very strong case for women's self-determination but in the same breath, she advanced the postulate that women, in order to be free, should not have children. This mode of argument proceeds in the following manner: the need for self-determination is established as the overriding one and, in order for it to be satisfied, certain *concrete* needs (in this case, having or not having children) are either discouraged or, eventually, imputed. Whilst this is an example of purely individual needs the same stricture applies to group decisions. For example, initiators of the process for self-determination in the sphere of public housing may well have a fairly clear picture in their minds of what kind of housing development would best suit people, and yet, if self-determination and hence free decision-making is to be taken seriously, the people affected ought decide even if their idea of the type of housing which best suits their needs is at variance with that of the initiators of the movement.

Distinguishing between the needs for self-determination and other needs and wants vested in all kinds of satisfiers is all the more important when one considers the impossibility of successfully mounting a case for self-determination without making a connection between the two groups of needs (with the only possible exception being self-determination in non-institutionalized relationships). One should bear in mind that want-orientated attitudes today are far more widespread than claims forged by needs for self-determination. It is not illusory to presume that needs for self-determination are, to a greater or lesser extent, present in the overwhelming majority of modern individuals but it is equally reasonable to assume that their satisfaction is sought indirectly, rather than directly, through the avenue of want-satisfaction. In the normal run of events, it is fair to say that people will exhibit a reluctance to participate in experiments for self-determination if they have reason to suspect that certain wants, in particular material ones, will not be met or even that they will not be met to the extent that they are at present. Self-determination itself, by definition, has to be self-determined and people are only likely to make claims for self-determination if they are convinced that their wants (except the needs for domination) will be met to the same extent and preferably to a higher degree than they are under existing conditions.

There are many other difficulties confronting those who participate in processes of self-determination. Existing institutions which make up the environment of the institution which people are attempting to change, could present enormous resistance to the changes which are envisaged by the sheer weight of their existence. Experiments for self-determination would not only stand a better chance of success, but would also gather momentum more easily, were such experiments supported and encouraged by other institutions. Political and social groupings could lend such support, as could the state, if sympathetic to the experiments. Furthermore, self-determination requires a heightened sense of responsibility, and it is also often very time-consuming. Many would simply not be prepared to take on such a responsibility or to sacrifice even a morsel of their leisure time. Besides, self-determination has its own economy. If a person is a member of several different groups and institutions, he/she can, and perhaps will, be ready to participate in the decision-making process of one, or even several of them, but certainly not in all of them; and yet the person might claim that his/her wants should be met in all of them. Space does not allow us to discuss other problems related to engaging in processes of self-determination and seeking the support of others to do likewise. Certain conclusions, however, can be drawn from what has been said thus far.

Those who seek self-determination have to cope with the context in which their actions are embedded, with the aim of widening the scope of self-determination. One can widen the scope of self-determination if one enters into a discursive relationship with others in a dialectical rather than in a rhetorical manner. One must distinguish between self-determination itself and the concrete wants people seek to satisfy, whether with or without discursive participation. One may solicit help and encouragement from other institutions (including the state), though one must ensure that such aid is not transformed into paternalism. The danger of this is particularly acute in the case of the state and some institutions whose principal functions are to act as guarantors for want-satisfaction alone. Decisions made by self-governed bodies can be criticized as can all needs and their corresponding satisfiers. However, in the case of a claim to self-determination, not only its underlying need but also its chosen course must receive full recognition. Finally, self-determination as a fundamental attitude does not call for active participation in every institution, nor every social and political group of which one is a member. Even a completely self-governed society, a society of radicalized democracy, could not possibly require of its members such all-round participation. For no society can be self-governed where the *need for non-participation* is not recognized. If such a need remains unrecognized, this would amount to a constraint on human needs which is itself detrimental to autonomy.

III

The question we have addressed at length here is how we can transform contingency into destiny while coping with our context. By way of conclusion, we would like to turn to two related problems. Firstly, the readiness to cope with our context in the way we have outlined and the satisfaction one gains from this process of coping are themselves conditioned. Secondly, coping with our context alone does not make us satisfied with our lives. Although 'being satisfied with our lives' does not presuppose the satisfaction of all our needs and wants, certain kinds of needs must indeed be satisfied before we can reach the point where we might be satisfied with our lives. Let us now turn briefly to these problems.

The condition which must be present for the readiness to cope with our context the way we have outlined is a simple one: one has to choose to be a decent person. To choose to be a decent, honest (or good) person requires the resolve that before embarking on an action, one will first check whether the particular action is right. A decent person gives priority to moral considerations as against considerations of a pragmatic kind (for example, which kind of action best serves one's particular interests). This does not mean that a decent person resigns from pursuing his/her own interests. The honest person will do this any time provided that pursuing one's own interest does not do injustice to other persons; that it does not wrong them. Indeed, we subscribe to Plato's definition of goodness: a good person is one who would sooner suffer an injustice (wrong) than commit an injustice (wrong). A good, decent or honest person of this kind is not a saint, nor is he/she an altruist. A good person does not seek suffering, nor does he/she seek being wronged. He/she accepts suffering, or being wronged, only in so far as the alternative to suffering injustice is being unjust or wronging others. It stands to reason why self-determination of the kind we have argued for in this chapter presupposes honesty and decency. If one does an injustice or wrong to others, one has violated the autonomy of others, one has withheld recognition of the needs of others, one has failed to co-operate with one's fellow creatures – in short, one has used others as mere means.

The type of needs which must certainly be satisfied before one could possibly be satisfied with one's own life is the need for practising one's ability to developing endowments into talents. Of course, we all have far more positive endowments than the ones we in fact develop into talents and we cannot possibly develop all our endowments into talents. Yet, in order to be satisfied with our lives we need to be satisfied that the endowments we have developed into talents were among the best.

The other types of needs which must be met are the ones for meaningful and deep attachments. If one or another personal attachment does not turn out the way we might have hoped it would, this, in itself, does not mean that we have not led a meaningful life. But if one has never had a single deep relation to any other person, one's life cannot be completely good.

Finally, there are great moments of complete fulfilment and delight, moments of happiness and rapture. Maslow termed such moments those of 'peak experience'. A life without a single peak experience is utterly miserable. It is also very rare: almost everyone has at least once, and often several times, enjoyed moments of fulfilment. Yet the more contingent a person is the more he/she will fall back into the experience of contingency in the aftermath of such an experience. A peak experience is for such a person the promise of a paradise which never materializes, the exception that has nothing to do with the rule, the moment that passes away without leaving any trace. Once the moment is gone, life becomes even more empty than it was before. Yet if the attitude of a person is rooted in the need for self-determination, peak experiences will not fade away. Springing as it does from life as a whole, and thus returning as it does into life as a whole, a peak experience can become an inspiration for the person, it can be 'caught' even if not perpetuated. To repeat: the attitude of self-determination operates like a *tonic*. It is due to this attitude that peak experience can impart flavour to all other experience. Metaphorically speaking: it makes life taste well. And indeed: the life we are satisfied with tastes well.

Notes

1 J. Habermas, *Der philosophische Diskurs der Moderne*, Suhrkamp, 1985.
2 A. Heller, *General Ethics* Oxford: Blackwell, 1988.
3 F. Fehér 'Redemptive and democratic paradigms in radical politics', in A. Heller and F. Fehér, *Eastern Left – Western Left* Cambridge: Polity Press, 1987.
4 For a more detailed elaboration of this view of modernity see A. Heller and F. Fehér, 'Class, democracy, modernity' in A. Heller and F. Fehér: *Eastern Left – Western Left*.

4

The Moral Situation in Modernity

I

Philosophers have always disagreed about the essence of human nature, the origins of morals and the interpretation of virtues and vices. As a result, they have tended to disagree about their moral recommendations. But when, conversely, it came to describing the moral status of the world, their agreement was overwhelming. Today, on the contrary, we have dozens of micro-communities, each of which speaks a different language as though they were communities belonging to different worlds. The moral symptoms one school refers to bear no likeness to the moral symptoms thematized by other micro-communities.

One particular discourse dissects our world in the terms of 'nihilism'. Participants in this discourse assume that there are no longer any valid norms, that virtues are gone and that on the one hand, persons act instrumentally while on the other hand they fit into external-institutional roles and requirements without having any intrinsic moral motivation at all. Another micro-discourse refers to this self-same world as the climax of moral development in so far as universal normative speech and moral rationality have gained momentum against irrational restraints, repressions and ethical tutelage. The third type of micro-discourse dismisses both the paradigm of nihilism and that of universalism–rationalism as equally empty talk which hold no bearing whatsoever to our own moral situation. Participants in this kind of discourse claim that liberal democracies maintain quite a healthy and vigorous moral life which is only mildly egoistic, fairly pragmatic and yet which is also public-issues orientated when it comes to *concrete* decisions concerning justice and injustice. We leave several other existing micro-discourses unmentioned because their impact does not transcend the lecture-halls of the academy. However, the impact of the three above-mentioned do. We consume our weekly dosage of Nietzsche and postmodernism with our Sunday breakfast as it is presented in our newspaper. During that same afternoon we will be involved in a heated discussion concerning affirmative action. In the evening, we will watch the picturesque images of world poverty on the television and begin to ponder how we might best be involved in remedies for that poverty. We are thus included within the framework of the discourse of nihilism to the same extent as in those of the healthy moral traditions of liberal democracy and universalistic rationalism.

And yet, the person who is exposed to this Sunday plethora of popularized philosophical experiences is *not* a nihilist at the breakfast table, a concerned, albeit mildly egoist, citizen in the afternoon and a universalistic rationalist by night. Perhaps he/she is a bit of the first, the second and the third or perhaps he/she understands, or at least is capable of understanding, his or her world in terms of all three micro-discourses. In what follows we would like to take the position of the innocent reader-listener and contend: all of the *symptoms* described by each of the three discourses are truly symptoms of the moral life of modern societies, and no one group of the symptoms is more decisive or overarching than the other two. Since the three discourses are competitive and mutually exclusive and since participants in one discourse would at best admit that the symptoms listed by others exist as *secondary* phenomena which have been mistakenly or wrongly elevated to the rank of basic features, and vice versa, our approach might appear at first glance to be eclectic. It is our intention to demonstrate that it is not.

II

Dostoevsky's *aperçu*: if God does not exist, everything is permitted, has been repeated ever since by almost all participants of the micro-discourse of 'nihilism'. This was so irrespective of whether they believed that the predicted outcome ('everything is permitted') is unavoidable for God is anyhow already dead, or whether they shared the hope that God could still be kept alive or resurrected, that he was only 'in eclipse', and thus that the moral world-order would, or at least might, escape total destruction. Dostoevsky's formula brings the central issue into focus and it is sharp and epigrammatic – perhaps this is why it is also misleading. If we take the *aperçu* 'everything is permitted' at its face value, it means that there are no moral norms and rules, neither concrete nor abstract; there are no regulations whatsoever and in the end therefore everyone does whatever he/she deems best for his or her own sake, be it interest or pleasure. It is obvious for everyone, and it must have been obvious for those underwriting the formula in the past, that a society in which 'everything is permitted' is simply impossible. Since social regulation is regulation by *rules*, there cannot be a single society in which everything is permitted for the infringement of rules is by definition, unpermitted. In a more pragmatic formulation this might read as follows: societies without ethical religions, lacking the image of a deity endowed with moral powers, can still have very dense systems of rule in the framework of which a large number of acts are disapproved, even severely punished. The formula of Dostoevsky must then mean something which has not been spelt out, only implied, and as such understood by people who share the same tradition. The tradition in question is the Christian one which includes significant moral elements of Judaism and Hellenism. Against this background, the 'Dostoevsky-formula' should be read as follows: 'If our (Christian) God does not exist, acts which have been prohibited in *our* moral tradition, will be permitted in the future'; and, one could add, acts which have been permitted, moreover, morally praised, may be prohibited in that future. It was exactly in this way that the 'Dostoevsky-dictum' was interpreted after the formidable experiences of Nazism and Stalinism. Not that Nazism and Bolshevism had 'permitted everything'. In fact both prohibited a wide range of activities, even ideas. To mention only one example, they morally disapproved of indulging in empathy with their victims or practising charity towards the wrong kind of people. At the same time, however, they permitted and even encouraged participation in ideologically underpinned, instrumentalized, mass murder which, in the spirit of our tradition, should have been prohibited. The real question therefore is not, as many firmly believed it was, that if God does not exist, we cannot tell good from evil. The real question is *what* shall we consider good, *what* evil.

If we read into the Dostoevsky-formula everything that has only been implied in the text, new questions immediately arise. If there is no God, in other words, if the transcendent guarantee and fountainhead of a traditional (Christian) morality loses its authority and spell, *what kind* of actions will be permitted? It was exactly this kind of inquiry which unfolded in modern rationalism. Reason became the authority of issuing permissions and underwriting traditional prohibitions. In the course of this 'change of authority', one prohibition after another became cancelled out and invalidated because they had been proven 'irrational', a prejudice or a mere fancy. The 'nihilism narrative' insists that this trend is unstoppable once reason takes the place of the dead God. This is allegedly the case since as soon as the validity of moral norms is no longer vouchsafed by the highest authority, the evildoer will ask you to give your reasons for refraining from deeds which he/she practices. You will give yours, he/she will give his or hers, and if argument is pitted against argument, no possibility of a moral decision can be reached. The decider is interest, force, comfort and conformity.

There is no need to describe modern times as the hotbed of moral 'nihilism' in order to face the problem which has given rise to the 'nihilism narrative'. All the serious modern moral philosophers have had their day of reckoning like our ancestor Jacob. If we do not notice the marks of the struggle on the body of their philosophy, this is only because they covered them up with alternative narratives. Although the paradigm of nihilism is normally associated with Nietzsche because he gave it a positive turn in the most radical way, the narrative had already made its appearance a hundred years earlier. The classic examples of reckoning with the sceptre of nihilism may be found in Diderot's *Rameau's Nephew* as well as in Kant's moral philosophy. Diderot's philosopher, the narrator of the dialogue, recognizes during the course of the discussion that the arguments of his interlocutor, the moral nihilist, are unbeatable. It only remains for him in defence of the case of goodness to express his *disgust* of the nihilist (an emotivist moral gesture) and to reaffirm his *own resolution* to be, and remain, a decent man, for it is better to be an honest person than a wicked clown. Of course, it cannot be rationally proven that it is better to be good than evil unless one can pinpoint absolute, eternal norms. And if one can, one does not need to prove anything. Diderot's work ends on the theme of an *existential choice of goodness*. In the absence of a God (and moral absolutes), one can still be good if, and only if, one chooses oneself as a good person. Without doubt, a choice like this is not rational because between all my reasons and my resolve there is the *leap*, as Kierkegaard was to point out later.

Kant check-mated nihilism while at the same time accepting every piece of nihilistic argumentation. If theoretical reason (speculation, calculation, argumentation) was supposed to precede action invalidating or devalidating norms, there was no longer any doubt in Kant's mind as to 'everything being permitted'. For the empirical man or woman, motivated by 'thirsts' of having, power and fame, would anyhow prove, and prove rationally, that whatever he/she desires is good. Theoretical reason does not provide certainty, and yet it is certainty which morals must be based on. But certainty eliminates choice. And how can one eliminate choice without backing away from modernity to traditional norms guaranteed by divine revelation? How can one preserve autonomy, personality and subjectivity without choice and at the same time reject understanding and knowledge as the source of validation or devalidation or moral norms? Kant has invented the most sophisticated, and almost flawless, philosophical answer to the new situation created by the increase in rationality on the one hand, and the discovery of the limits to reason on the other. As is well known, the whole edifice of the Kantian solution rests on his dual anthropology. Eliminate noumenal man and you will arrive at modern nihilism pure and simple. Eliminate phenomenal man and you will arrive at speculative formal universalism from which the actor is absent. Should one reject Kant's dual anthropology for any theoretical or empirical reason (including introspection and value-preferences), the fragile balance between certitude and relativism will be upset.

Hegel, who had his own days of reckoning, made the heroic effort to rebuild and refurbish inner-worldly ethical authority named *Sittlichkeit*; he knew, much as Diderot and Kant had previously known, that pinpointing an existing *sittlich* world-order with the gesture: 'here it is, these are the norms and rules to follow', will not suffice. For the addressee will certainly retort by asking the inquisitive question, 'why is that so?' 'why should I observe the norms of this particular world-order and not those of other ones, or none at all?' Hegel believed, much as Kant, that in order to fight nihilism (and, he added, empty subjectivism), the *sittlich* order must shine in the light of absolute certitude. Hegel could make a case for a more relaxed, elastic and complex moral universe, for more liberalism and more leniency, because the basic groundwork of his ethical edifice was erected in a fixed and rigid manner. World history, he contended, this supreme judge, had led humankind to its present state, the World Spirit itself presents us with the outcome of its own long wandering. Yet such a balance is again utterly fragile. Curtail the emphasis on *Sittlichkeit* while maintaining the grand narrative alone, and you will get an objective teleology in which the ethical content of subjective telos is of no relevance whatsoever. The result of this amputation is that everything which supposedly furthers the development of world history will indeed be permitted, and nihilism reconfirmed. Or conversely, eliminate the world-historical narrative, while maintaining the emphasis on *Sittlichkeit*, and you will arrive at a pragmatism of a kind in which certain modern rules of the game are taken for granted without more ado.

The solution of existential choice (Diderot's impasse) does not require the backing of any particular metaphysics, ontology, system, speculative edifice or anthropology. However, both Kant's and Hegel's respective solutions, and to the same extent, must be backed up or even founded by complete systems. Philosophically they are convincing but amidst the vicissitudes of modern morals these complete systems cause more problems than they can solve. But there are perhaps other avenues to be explored.

Derrida embarked on a voyage which did not seem to be worth the while: deconstructing a seemingly rather insignificant paper written by Kant in 1796 (*Von einem neuerdings erhobenen vornehmen Ton in der Philosophie*). From our perspective, it is not the parody of Kant's utterly pedantic approach to something essentially unpedantic which is of relevance to us, nor even the apocalyptic allusions unearthed from under Kant's silence by Derrida, but rather the way in which Derrida magnifies what he terms Kant's gesture of reconciliation. In brief, Kant mounts an unusually vitriolic attack (unusual given his mild standards) against mystical Platonists, who are abused by him as *mystagogue-eschatologists*, and in particular against Schlosser who is accused by Kant of castrating philosophy, and almost finishing off the enterprise. The real surprise arrives at the end: the conclusion of the paper is the recommendation that he, Kant, and his contemptible philosophical enemies should work together for the same purpose. We all want to make human beings decent, he insists, and we all want to serve the moral law. Whatever our respective philosophies might be, we could venture this supreme task together. We think that this small pedantic piece of writing by an old and declining man, this awkward gesture towards alien philosophical tastes and interests is absolutely wonderful and heroic. The attempt to accept the modern condition of theoretical pluralism with the proviso that all philosophers should work for the same practical purpose (more decency, obedience to the moral law) is not merely an exercise in liberal tolerance, it also expresses a new *philosophical insight*. We know that Kant needed his dual anthropology, in particular the fact of reason, in order to prove the existence of moral law, although it could not in fact be proven in terms of his own philosophical conviction either. He needed it in order to make a case for certainty, the absolute, the categorical; to be able to dismiss choice, even the choice of the self, the risk, the leap. When he therefore conceded that the cause of moral reason, of moral law, can be furthered, presented and represented by completely different philosophers, those philosophies were grounded in different types of metaphysics, in different ontologies and anthropologies, with this same gesture he resigned the tenet that the work of practical reason in the world can be grounded in a fully rational way. For this new position it now sufficed simply to assert that those who did not ground goodness completely rationally, as Kant did, could still, however, work for the same moral purpose. With this gesture, the philosophical grounding of morals has already been relativized. From this we would derive our preliminary conclusion: it is ill conceived to establish a direct relation between the increasing relativism of world-views (philosophies) and the relativism of morals. Perhaps the opposite is the case: through absolutizing their own philosophies and world-views, philosophers contribute more to the relativization of morals, even to boosting nihilism, than by the acceptance of the mutual relativization of their philosophical enterprises, by finding only a single and restricted common ground: a few moral norms and values which might be regarded as valid and binding for all of us.

The diversity of world-views, philosophies, metaphysics and religious faiths does not bar the emergence of a common ethos, unless one of the competing world views completely determines the commandments and the interdictions, and does so not only for its own adherents but also with a universalizing aspiration.

III

The categorical figures of 'the whole and the part', as well as the 'one– several–many' had first made their appearance as moral, political and metaphysical configurations at the time of the birth of philosophy. Another metaphysical, and logical, figure, 'the universal, the singular and the particular', have become heavily politicized in the new age and also applied to morals. In structural terms, the singular proved the least problematic element of the triad. There was no contender for this position other than the single individual, the person *qua* actor, *qua* moral (responsible) subject. The universal turned out to be the most problematic element of the triad. In a universal proposition, the same is predicated about all (same) cases. If therefore 'the single individual' is the singular, it follows that 'individual as such', that is, 'all individuals' should be the universal. But this never eventuated in actual moral discourse. The position of the universal has been occupied by the notion 'humankind' which is itself polysemic and which can denote shades of meaning other than the universal equivalent of all singular individuals. Or, even worse, this position has been occupied by any category of integration which encompasses (either hierarchically or structurally, or both senses) several human integrations which are no longer polysemic but not simply equivalent to 'all individuals'. For how can entities such as 'the state' be identified with the universal? In order to substitute the state for 'all individuals', one must supply a new singular for 'the single individual'. This new singular is no longer 'the human being' but the 'single citizen' or 'the single German, French, etc.'. We thus have a moral agent, alias the 'single individual' whose relation to the universal (humankind, all human agents) is mediated by the particular (e.g. the state), and we have a moral agent (termed 'single citizen', 'the French', 'the German', etc.) who relates to a universal (the state) which, for him or her as a human being, is not a universal at all, or at least not meant to be such. One of the most serious problems and dilemmas of modern morals is encapsulated in this seemingly semantic–logical dilemma.

The new occidental philosophy, as it had taken shape by the seventeenth century, deduced moral facts (norms, ideas, obligations, images of the right and the good) from a few anthropological assumptions, that is, from certain 'eternal' attributes of human nature in general. An abstract and a historical anthropological universalism vouched for the explanation for the genesis. As far as this genesis was concerned, the propensities of each and every person were the Propensities of Man (of all humankind), as such and it was only the social contract which was believed to engender moral duties and obligations of a proper (and concrete) kind. The citizen, as the singular appertaining to the general, 'the state', was ethically related to the state. However, the individual human being, as a human being, could not be related to all human beings (its own universal) with any kind of ethical ties, for 'all human beings' did not, and still does not, constitute any integration whatsoever. As a result there were no obligations or duties which the singular were bound to heed due to their membership in the human race. Instead of being properly related to its own universal, the singular termed 'person' or 'human being' was now related to civil society and the family. These integrations were considered more particularistic than the state, not only for Hegel, but also for Hobbes, Locke and Rousseau. In a strict philosophical sense, Marx was right when he claimed that 'man' is tantamount to the bourgeois, because the single human person whose duties and obligations (in so far as he/she has any) are exclusively to his/her business and his/her family is precisely the bourgeois. Yet the claim to be related, in a positive sense and therefore also morally, 'to all humans', or 'to humankind' or 'to the human essence' above and beyond all particularistic obligations and determinations, has also made its appearance. A certain kind of secularized (or almost secularized) Christianity, sometimes in the form of Freemasonry, became merged with the concerns of modern theories of natural law. This is the tendency which we will refer to as 'modern humanism'. In our opinion, humanism is not identical with the Cartesian legacy of subjectivism; neither is it co-terminous with the venture to place the individual person at the centre of the universe. Humanism does not stand for leniency, for *tout comprendre, c'est tout pardonner*; nor does it stand for the attempt to make all of our moral norms and rules rational. There is an element of subjectivism in humanism but not of the epistemological kind. If someone takes upon himself or herself certain duties and obligations on behalf of an entity (humankind) which does not exist, the subjective aspect of ethics (morality) will unquestionably be more present in such a gesture than in the same person's relation to existing integrations with a dense ethical substance. In a direct commitment to the universal there is a strong element of a certain kind of rationality, which we have termed 'the rationality of intellect'. This is particularly so if the self-imposed duties to a non-existing entity collide with duties imposed by existing entities; for the person living amidst such a collision, unless he/she remains on the level of a mere gesture, normally gives reasons for preferring the universal to the particular. Yet modern humanism such as the kind exemplified by Lessing, does not centre around the single person. Rather, there is a touch of mysticism in modern humanism, a commitment to some kind of common mana dwelling in all of us irrespective of our nationalities, affiliations, religious commitments, metaphysical creeds and beliefs. This mana makes us turn towards each other as we suspend our particular affiliations, without abandoning or resigning them; a mana which furthermore we do not lose except in the event of an ultimate moral transgression.

Thinking in terms of 'rights' has gained prominence simultaneously with modern humanism. Modern humanism embraced 'right-thinking' as the negative aspect of its own vision. Attributing 'inalienable' rights to members of an integration on the basis of their personhood could be considered as the single greatest contribution of liberal theories to the development of modern *Sittlichkeit*. Modern humanism simply must subscribe to the liberal norm of the rights of humanity. For if all particularist determinations are to be suspended in our intercourse with other humans *qua* humans, then every single individual being has to be protected against the force, pressure and interference of particularist integrations (determinations). Thus modern humanism comprises 'right-thinking', but it also has both different and broader connotations. The enthusiastic gesture of *seid umschlungen, Millionen* cannot be equated with the defence of human rights.

It is in Kant's moral philosophy that all these threads were tied together in a philosophically conclusive way. He shifted both the individual and the particular on to the side of the recipient, assuming that they will put up resistance while receiving the universal message. As members of the rational world, we are universal, as members of the empirical world, we are particular and single entities; the moral law, humankind as such and humankind in us, is the universal. Finally, the particular (the constitution of the republic, or the legal-ethical, though not moral, world) is to be related to the universal. It becomes clear from Kant's way of arguing that if all constitutions are good, then they are all also completely alike, and that in the world republic (or Commonwealth), in the sign of the eternal peace, all constitutions and political arrangements must in fact be alike. Finally, Kant makes a concession to the particular and the individual, especially in his *Metaphysics of Morals*, but it is only a minor one.

Hegel accused Kant of being guilty of neglecting the particular and the individual. The freedom of particularity and the well-being of the individual rests in pluralism. 'Civil society', the sphere which comprises particularity in the modern age, consists of a variety of institutions, integrations, corporations, professions and the like. Each of them develops its own intrinsic *Sittlichkeit*. The state is tantamount to the universal. The moral order of the state warrants the universality (generality) of all the particularities emerging around the institutions of civil society. The individual having attained the highest form of subjectivity, subjects himself or herself to his/her corporation relatively, but he/she does so to the state completely for supreme *Sittlichkeit* demands *Einordnung in das Allgemeine* which in English means fitting oneself properly into generality/universality, that is, the state. So, the modern state is the main source of *Sittlichkeit*, because it is the universal – but which modern state? There are several states, and

Hegel appreciated the wars among them also from an ethical point of view. If all modern states represent universality by definition, then the universal is the particular, and the particular is only termed universal. If two countries wage war against each other, is there never and nowhere any *criteria* to decide whose case is just, whose is unjust, whose case is *more* just or more *right* than the other? If there is no answer to this question, then complete relativism is the end result. The universalism of the world spirit will then result in the simultaneity of unmediated yet conflicting particularities which claim absolute loyalty from the individuals because they all identify themselves as the universal.

Modern humanism was lofty but it did not provide the modern world with visible bonds, with a set of transparent norms; in other words: *Sittlichkeit*. Instead, nationalism has supplied them. Precisely as Hegel predicted, it happened in war that the brute egoism of the 'spiritual animal kingdom' was overcome. It was the experience of totalitarianism which made the identification of the particular (a state) with the universal (humankind, the end result of human history, etc.) deeply suspect. Although 'nation' has remained the major object of moral commitment, more so than ever in fact, especially given that whole continents joined the choir of nationalism and jingoism, moral theory and philosophy has been forced to explore the possibilities and realities in other directions.

All these directions can be seen as recycled versions of the answers already given to the dilemma some two hundred years ago. 'Recycled' does not stand here for the statement that the questions, or the inquiries into the answers, are actually identical. Obviously the experiences of two hundred years have been digested, reflected upon and expressed. The word 'recycling' refers rather to the types of answer and the tendencies they represent. Modern humanism, especially in its Kantian version, is again with us and it has come to its fruition in the theory of communicative ethics. In the framework of the latter, individuals raise *truly* universal claims, not simply claims which are in fact particular and only termed universal. This stand also implies that we have once again relapsed into Kantian formalism, and that the dense ethics of *Sittlichkeit*, though mentioned and referred to, are not reflected upon in a positive manner. Practical reason becomes the twin of theoretical reason, for *phronesis* (prudence) has disappeared from the horizon. Something similar could be stated of self-professed Kantians like Bair, Singer, Gerth, Gewirth and the others. Whereas in Hegel all particularities were believed to lead towards the highest one termed universal, namely the state, the modern types of discourse revert back to the category of the individual. There is such a great variety of this 'language game', to use a favorite term of these Kantians, that only certain salient types can be mentioned. Closest to Hegel remains the discourse that dominates the philosophy of American liberalism. For Rawls, Dworkin, Ackerman *et alii* the state is identical with the constitution, and the ethos of human co-operation is to be sought in a constitution which is fair, and thus right. Human right, the main property of every person, is understood as the right of the citizen. It is assumed that human beings who are well-endowed with rights (liberties) conduct their business with one another while respecting the liberties of others within the framework of this self-same constitution. The most recent writings of Walzer and Rorty make a plea for a thick contextuality, in the framework of which every participant in public affairs knows what the whole framework is all about and where everyone shares the rules of an ethical world and takes them for granted.

In our brief overview of theoretical reflection upon the relationship between the members of the triad (particular–universal–individual) at the dawn of the modern age, we did not mention the radical shift in the direction of the individual. Of course, almost everything appears sporadically before it becomes truly representative. After certain romantic precursors, Kierkegaard is the first philosopher who looks for the source of morality in the individual (in the individual's existential choice of himself or herself) without identifying the object (territory, sphere) of moral practice with its source. The individual *qua* individual *is* the universal, yet the territory of moral life is to be sought in interpersonal relations (including particularity). The discourse initiated by Kierkegaard need not be recycled because it has been continuously if not always conspicuously present in our modern age.

IV

In the first paragraph we mentioned three typical diagnoses of the contemporary moral condition. We have added that they are all in a sense correct. In the second paragraph we put the paradigm of nihilism under closer scrutiny and dissected the items belonging under this heading. At that point, two conclusions could be drawn. Firstly, the dangers which have been discovered within the paradigm of nihilism are not pre-empted by the assumption that the diagnoses of the other two paradigms are also correct. Secondly, it is not pluralism but rather the claim to absolutism which prevents competing metaphysics and philosophies from finding a common moral ground. In the third paragraph, we continued to present the very issue which in our view lies at the heart of division of modern moral philosophy. We have added that the decisive division is backed by life experiences, and that the same division has been recycled for two hundred years, and in some cases even more. This circumstance alone should make us suspicious not only of too straightforward and unilinear narratives of ethical progression or moral decay, but also of the self-complacency of the discourse of 'the healthy moral traditions of liberal democracy'. Neither in the case of an increasing moral decay nor under the conditions of a vigorous moral progression, nor, finally, under the auspices of the smooth operation of the modern tradition, would the same theoretical configuration be recycled again and again. If viewed from this position all apocalyptic statements cut a fairly comic figure. We have heard so often for such a long time that we are 'right-at-the-beginning-of' or, alternatively, that we are 'right-at-the-end-of' the 'real thing', that apocalyptic language has become everyday language for common use. But there is equally a touch of the comical in the conviction that those who learn to take a positive stand on affirmative action have already solved the major moral problems of our time.

The simultaneous process of universalization, particularization and individualization is equivalent to the appearance of contingency as the condition of the modern world. If there is no World Spirit with its inherent telos, then history as world history is itself contingent; so are all particularities constituted by, or unfolding within, this history. It is above all the individual, the person, who becomes contingent, and who knows himself or herself, understands his/her world and situation as such. When discussing individuals in so far as they are 'situated', a current figure of speech in modern moral philosophy, we have in mind the contingent individual person. In recycling the old questions and theoretical figures, which is unavoidable within the same world-historical epoch, moral philosophies of the present will have to concentrate on the modern human condition, which is one of contingency, in order to shape a moral philosophy that will apply to a contingent person.

The re-birth of Aristotle's moral philosophy, the emergence of a certain type of neo-Aristotelian moral philosophy can also be understood from this perspective. Aristotle's moral philosophy summed up and recycled, in a way, all the questions and answers which had been previously posed and formulated in such slightly different cultures as the Athenian, the Ionian and others. In as far as it was possible in a fairly static world, Aristotle made an inventory of the plurality of *Sittlichkeit*, of the diversities of personal tastes, of the possible difference between the good citizen and the good person, to the differentiation of *techne* from action. In addition, he, unlike Plato, 'settled in', so to speak, with his moral and political philosophy. Aristotle came after the Greek Enlightenment; he made an inventory of the potentials of, and the limits to, reason and finally he offered a fair combination of formal with substantive ethics.

Neo-Aristotelians, at least some of them, look for a model in the philosophy of the Stagirite in order to contrast it with the alleged contemporary moral decay. Others, like Castoriadis and Arendt, are more eager to discover similarities between our problems and his than to oppose the ancient (read: authentic) with the modern (read: the decadent). If we depart from Aristotle's moral philosophy, we will indeed find stark contrasts to, and great similarities with, our modern moral world and moral thinking. The main line of division between Aristotle's perception of morals and ours resides in the absence and presence of contingency. Even if his relation to his world was relatively detached, Aristotle's moral political individual was far from being contingent. He was not 'situated', he was what he was, and could not have been anybody else. If he had been anyone else, he would not have had a place in Aristotle's ethics at all. Because contingency is not a philosophical construct which could be replaced by any other constructs but the life experience of the modern individual, a vexing, threatening but also promising experience (termed by Kierkegaard the experience of possibility or anxiety), a moral philosophy such as Aristotle's which remains unaffected by, or non-cognizant of, this matter, necessarily falls short of authentic contemporaneity.

The impossibility of coming to agreement on the description of moral facts in modern life simply follows from the ontological grounding situation of contingency. This is why an attempt at agreement has hardly any chance. The recurring complaint that philosophers are 'one-sided', that they miss this or that equally existing or perhaps all-important aspect of life, is a modern complaint. At the same time, it is a pointless one. One need not discover oneself, one's own environment and situation, one's own feeling and concern in each and every contemporary philosophy. One can absorb a philosophy as the expression of the life experience of another person who is as contingent as we are.

However, no moral relativism necessarily follows from this. The circumstance that my life experiences are expressed in this philosophy, those of another in another philosophy, does not transform or degrade philosophies themselves into idle games. Apart from the desire and the resolve to transform our own contingency into our own destiny – whatever our contingencies are – we also have common business to attend to.

After a long detour we are back at the concluding problems of the second paragraph, back to Kant's awkward gesture of reconciliation, in order to make a common cause for morals, for practical reason.

Particular moral worlds are different in kind, whether they are religious, communal, co-operative, political or whatever. To create 'harmony' among the heterogeneity of *Sittlichkeit*, or even to make the different kinds of *Sittlichkeit* equally dense or equally loose, is an enterprise which is doomed to failure in the contemporary world. (The world might, however, change but morals are concerned less with prophecy than any other material of our speculation.) The modern individual (the singular) is contingent in every *Sittlichkeit*, yet he/she can choose himself or herself as well as he/she can fall short of choosing, can be a person of conscience as much as not, can be authentic as much as inauthentic within the framework of each and every particular world. But what about the universal? Every world can offer different explanations of the origins of good and evil, of the goodness or wickedness of our race, yet it is the universal gesture, not the universalistic explanation, that matters. By universal gesture we mean participation in what has been termed the attitude of modern humanism. Doing something in our capacity as 'human beings as such', doing it for others as for 'human beings as such', doing it together with others, in symmetric reciprocity, solidarity, friendship as 'human beings as such' – this is the meaning of 'universal gesture'. It is irrelevant from which source one draws the strength to do these things for what matters most is that one *does* such things. Humankind is not a universal cluster, it has not worked out its *Sittlichkeit*. Yet there are certain kinds of action which we all know are right, good, desirable, and commendable. Moral philosophies may make a case for such gestures. They can also ponder further, even remote, possibilities for the emergence of certain universalistic moral ties.

We have mentioned several times that men and women of modernity are recycling old themes and old solutions, albeit in new orchestrations and variations; the first formulations of the concerns of modern moral philosophy are roughly two hundred years old. The universal gesture, which is far from dependent on the universal explanation, has been traced back to the old age of Kant. However, the idea that moral universalism can be achieved not by surpassing contingency, particularity and individuality, but rather by changing our attitude within one and the same form of life, goes back to Lessing, and has been recycled by Hannah Arendt. If the process of recycling is to continue, sooner or later a fourth type of main discourse may emerge which would join the discourses of nihilism, formal universalism and concrete particularism. This new type of discourse refers back to the contingent individual as its starting point, not to the hero, the genius, the role-player or the one-dimensional puppet, but to a person like you, or us.

5

Political Principles

Our analysis here will not comprise the morphology of various branches of present-day pragmatic politics which remain unaffected by theories and ideas, the exclusive aims of which are circumscribed by the exigencies of obtaining and staying in power. Nor is our objective to discuss the modern types of Machiavellian theory which propose to understand politics as *technique*. (In this context it will suffice to remark that Machiavellism has never been implemented in practice in any sustained political project, though of course, within particular circumstances its principles have been employed from time to time – particularly in circumstances analogous to those envisaged by Machiavelli himself, when a freshly conquered power has had to secure itself.) Finally, we have one further caveat. We shall touch only briefly on the equally extreme proposal that politics should be based on morality, and we shall reject it.[1]

A political principle regulates *all* political actions; that is to say, no action taken should contradict the principle. Yet political principles do not define single political actions: there are normally more options than one in each and every case. Particular situations have to be well understood, well assessed, optimal solutions have to be sought; in short, pragmatic considerations arise legitimately within the framework set by a principle, but the former should *never* override the latter. The principle lends coherence to all political actions; the politician who operates with principles is not 'politicking' but is engaging in genuine political activity, whether right or wrong.

Weber rejected the view that politics are based on morality (the so-called ethics of ultimate ends or *Gesinnungsethik* in politics) and recommended other political ethics, the so-called 'ethics of responsibility'.[2] The highest, at the same time the only, moral obligation of the politician is to find out the foreseeable consequences of his/her actions and to take responsibility for them. The message is clear enough: Kantian morality has no place in politics where the realities of the world are frequently at odds with the politician's own beliefs; it thus is incumbent upon the politician to measure his/her actions according to the results they are likely to engender and to be prepared to meet the unintended consequences of any action. Even if we believe (with Aristotle and Hegel) that reckoning with the foreseeable consequences of an action is a general duty applicable to all action, and not politics alone, it nevertheless seems reasonable to suggest that this duty has greater relative weight in political action. Common sense may also suggest that it is so by virtue of the scope and quantity of consequences which not only affect the actor and his/her close environment but all members of an institution, a group, a nation, and eventually all humankind.

Yet quantity alone cannot account for such moral distinctions. We would therefore rather differentiate between two kinds of responsibility which, for the present purposes, we shall call 'Responsibility X' and 'Responsibility A'. 'Responsibility X' means that one is responsible for acting in accordance with general duties, norms and rules (or for infringing them). However, it is not only the infringement of norms that can harm others. Thus one is not only obliged to observe norms but also to apply them with good judgement (which Aristotle called *phronesis*) to various situations, persons, and the like. If one fails in one's judgement, one is responsible for the harm thus caused, in other words, for the consequences of one's actions. 'Responsibility A' includes other commitment not included in 'Responsibility X'. It is equivalent to 'being in charge'. In such situations one takes responsibility for all those being, so to speak, in one's charge. The captain of a ship is in charge of the passengers; therefore he/she is responsible for the lives and security of his/her passengers. This is his/her responsibility and it is not the responsibility of each and every passenger. The obverse side of it is that everyone is obliged to observe general duties but no one is obliged to become a captain. Similarly, in the case of the politician. If someone volunteers to act on behalf of others (which is what being a politician entails), he/she put himself or herself 'in charge'. Should the political vessel be wrecked, he/she will be fully responsible for the shipwreck. Similarly, safe sailing will be to his/her credit.

So far we have supported the Weberian 'ethic of responsibility' with further arguments but it is here that our agreement ends. For the 'ethic of responsibility' cannot answer the crucial question concerning which consequences are good (desirable) and which are bad (undesirable). Of course, one could dismiss this objection as completely irrelevant with the following, well-known argument: politics is a power game, therefore the consequences are by definition good if the might of the body politic in question (the state, nation) has been increased as a result of a particular action. An immediate rejoinder to this is that 'good' consequences for 'our' state could be devastating for others and it is not easy to see on what grounds we can exclude our effects on others from the assessment of political action. As soon as we cease to see politics simply in terms of a one nation-centred power game, the position of the 'ethic of responsibility' becomes even more shaky. To do justice to Weber we must remember that he did not equate the 'ethic of responsibility' with *Realpolitik*.[3] But in our view Weber's conception of political responsibility is unable to deal with the complexity of political action. Weber pinpointed the eventual devastating consequences of adhering in politics to an ethic of ultimate ends, in which one would pursue the ultimate end of the 'redemption of mankind' and judge all means deemed necessary to attain this objective as equally legitimate. While we agree with his final verdict here, we feel that Weber glosses over certain crucial questions. To begin with, *for whom* would the results really be devastating and from which point of view? Certain they would be devastating for those who took the ultimate end seriously and conceived it as a commitment, rather than as a mere legitimizing ideology. At the same time, they would not be devastating at all, but rather the 'natural costs of a social experiment', for those employing the ultimate end as a *ruse de guerre* or a non-binding statement of goodwill. Lukács, the main target of Weber's criticism, would not for one single moment have approved of the consequences of the Bolshevik political ethics of 'ultimate ends', had he been able to foresee them.[4] However, Bela Kun, an equally representative figure of early communism, would certainly have not disapproved of those consequences (with the exception of his own execution in 1938!) He despised ethics (which he called 'communist theology') and had no feeling for the lives of others in the world-historical experiment. In the same vein *all* Soviet leaders who have survived Stalin's purges approve the consequences of Stalin's actions, fully, rather than partially; Khrushchev was an important exception. (Gorbachev belongs to a new generation.) Therefore when Weber declared (and forecast) the consequences of pursuing an 'ethic of ultimate ends' he departed from his own method. He *knew* (because he had defined them substantively in advance) which were desirable and which were undesirable consequences. In fact, Weber himself made his own decision *not* from the position of his own theory, the 'ethic of responsibility', but from the position of a *political (and moral) principle* which he believed to be *valid*, and not simply successful.

Let us clarify this further. Taking responsibility for consequences presupposes a *prior* distinction between good and bad consequences and this can only happen on a basis *other* than that of the 'ethic of responsibility'. At this stage, our earlier metaphor of the captain being in charge of his/her ship becomes inadequate. Given the nature of the undertaking, every qualified captain *knows* (there are precise and relatively simple criteria for such knowledge) which are the good and which are the bad consequences of his/her action. Politics are, however, much more complex than navigation. Even if politics are about good judgement, they are not reliant on exact criteria. Whether an increase in equality or inequality is a 'good' consequence, whether victory in a war is better than a sensible compromise, whether assimilation is preferable to the dissimilation of an ethnic group; all these are questions which have to be decided *substantively* and *prior* to political action in order that we might be able to know which kind of actions might lead to good or bad consequences. In other words, without established principles for political action no responsibility for political action can be taken.

In the aftermath of World War Two a few politicians acted very much in the spirit of the Weberian ethic of responsibility. De Gaulle stands out among them in character and achievement, precisely because he interpreted the ethic of responsibility in the only way that it can be interpreted without self-contradiction. For him the substantive definition of good consequences was tantamount to increasing the might of his own country. He never once doubted that whatever served to increase the political might of France was a good consequence, nor that he, and he alone, knew what would serve France well (for *he was France*). While De Gaulle was the greatest practitioner of the politics (and ethics) of responsibility, Kissinger was, and has remained, its best theorist in a post-World War Two environment. Since he could not implement his politics in full, we can only refer the reader to his books which will clearly show the Weberian character and origin of his thinking. The following comprise the main features of Kissinger's political theory.

1   A politician must not raise any substantive goals.
2   The 'moralizing' or 'sentimental' streak of previous American policy making has to be discarded. Not shaking hands with totalitarian statesmen (the allusion to the famous Dulles-Chou En-lai episode is clear) whose morality we loathe is an impermissible basis for the conduct of politics. Moralistic politics is dangerous, and it cannot even be conclusive. It perforce vacillates between isolationism, on the one hand, and over-commitment, on the other hand.
3   Good politics have only one criterion: beneficial consequences.
4   What are the beneficial consequences under present-day circumstances? World politics are a chess-board. The two players are the Soviet Union and the United States. 'Beneficial consequences' can therefore be described in the following terms: any politician who makes the moves for the United States, has to improve its situation on the chess-board. However, a check-mate move is excluded from the game since any attempt to enforce it would lead to devastating consequences for the United States as well.
5   Nuclear showdown (the possible result of a check-mate) can only be avoided if the powers play the game with a relative sincerity. One can avoid a check-mate (which is tantamount to the destruction of both partners) if one does not aim at 'snatching' the other's sphere of influence. The balance between the two spheres of influence has to be kept such that the United States should try to increase its sphere of influence slightly in the awareness that the USSR will aim at the same result and vice versa.
6   'Relative sincerity' can be achieved via continuous contact and consultation between the two superpowers. It is only via continuous consultation that one can possibly find out what new move, if any, is being contemplated by the other in order to pre-empt it through an appropriate counter-move. One should never disclose any intended move to the other party *in full* for this would risk being out-manouevred, though one could hint at the possibility of such a move in order to be able to enter into a bargaining position. But there must be a clear awareness in advance of the impossibility of *check-mate*, whatever the intended move. Kissinger has no illusions: half the world is already communist; for him it only matters that the other half remains non-communist.

This is a clear-cut case of the political ethic of responsibility. Kissinger takes account of the optimal good consequences of political action from one point of view: the might of the United States under present-day circumstances. This is indeed an *ethic* of responsibility for the politician must not gamble. He/she has to be aware of the fact that the *optimal* is not identical with the *maximal*. Just the contrary: should a leader set himself or herself the task of maximizing the might of the United States (which can only happen through a nuclear showdown), such action can only lead to consequences devastating for the USA as well. And it is precisely the conclusive and sincere application of the 'ethic of responsibility' which clearly demonstrates the limitations of this ethic and supports our initial thesis that acting in accordance with this ethic in an international context ultimately means an increase of the might of a particular country and this alone can be the meaning of this ethic. However, to fully understand Kissinger's position we must examine one further dimension.

7   Given that according to Kissinger, two players engage in the chess game called world politics, all other countries are pawns on the chess-board. The greatest obstacle to the implementation of the political ethic of responsibility is, to use Kissinger's word, the *intransigence* of the pawns on the chess-board. For politics to be successful in Kissinger's terms, both superpowers have to keep their own allies in check. This is a matter of the gravest concern as allies often have a will of their own, and it is very difficult to make them comply with the moves of the superpowers, but yet this is required in a 'relatively sincere' game. Kissinger complains bitterly about Israel's intransigence (a problem for America), and he believes that the USSR is equally bitter about the continuous intransigence of Iraq or Syria. We already know that for Kissinger the scope of possible manoeuvres is limited by the existence of the two spheres of influence which must not be touched. The partners play in a 'fair' way if they do not try to 'snatch' units from the other sphere of influence, though they may from the pool of non-aligned countries. For Kissinger, the outcome of the political development in Cuba was the result of 'foul play', but the invasion of Czechoslovakia must be regarded as 'fair play' by the Soviet Union. Thus Kissinger subscribes to the Brezhnev doctrine: the borders of Czechoslovakia are, for him as much as for Brezhnev, the border of the USSR.[5]

In this view of the world, alliance becomes simply a geopolitical matter. The wills of nations which occupy certain positions on the globe thus cannot, and should not, be taken into consideration. Of course, Kissinger knows perfectly well that geopolitical considerations have nothing to do with justice; nor does he pretend that they do. He is aware that certain countries within the American geopolitical sphere of influence tend to a kind of radicalism (to the change of elites) which could lead them to forging a commonality of interests with the Soviet Union designed to bring about change. He also has no illusions whatsoever as to the east-European countries' desire to be rid of their dependence on the USSR, to be non-aligned or often the allies of the United States. Moreover, Kissinger as a social theorist does not believe in 'conspiracy' theories (which was obviously no obstacle to the Secretary of State using the CIA for purposes clearly circumscribed by his political 'ethic of responsibility'). He is always aware of the *internal* causes of intransigence, upheavals, rebellions and revolutions, should they happen in any sphere of influence. But at the same time, he declares more appropriate or equitable internal arrangements to be irrelevant form the viewpoint of responsible politics. All internal changes, in his line of argument, bring about *automatic*, and sometimes very drastic, changes in the balance of powers and this is why they are dangerous and can lead to devastating consequences irrespective of the just or unjust character of the cause they are expressions of. Justice and injustice are *substantive goals* (ultimate ends), and thus the politician who acts according to an 'ethic of responsibility' must exclude them from consideration.

To do justice to Kissinger, his politics are still better than day-to-day pragmatism, and are superior to politics based on an 'ethic of ultimate ends': if consistently implemented they can prevent us from reaching the brink of a nuclear Holocaust. However, as self-consciously conservative-restorative politics, they are structurally incompatible with the pursuit of democratic politics of any provenance. Politics based on an ethic of responsibility must take the status quo for granted for the simple reason that political actors who see change, must know in advance the good and the bad consequences of their actions, and these can only be decided under the guidance of *principle other* than 'responsibility'. This is why politics based on the ethic of responsibility are not only deeply anti-democratic, but also limited in their objective. As the status quo has to be taken for granted, the objective must be negative in nature: avoiding the worst and seeking success only within the framework of 'avoidance'. Responsibility for any positive outcome of the present world situation in accordance with the wills, the needs and desires of nations and regions, is excluded by definition.

Apart from the democratic, there are also other types of politics which seek to change the status quo, and a certain contingent of the left, sadly, remains entangled in them. At this point, there is no reason to weaken the validity and topicality of Weber's argument: non-democratic politics aimed at social change can only lead to devastating consequences which might still otherwise be avoided by the pursuit of non-democratic politics based on an ethic of responsibility. It is at this juncture that the decisive question has to be raised: are there principles for conclusive democratic politics? Are there principles which, if observed and implemented in practice, would make it possible to cope with the dual demands of political action: namely, the avoidance of a final showdown (which today would indeed be final) and to change our world for the better, in co-operation with all the people we share this world with. Behind this question lies the firm conviction that while politics based on an 'ethic of responsibility' may prevent us from utter destruction in the short run, they are certainly ineffectual in the long run. Only consistently democratic politics could achieve final and irreversible disarmament because it would not only maintain the balance of nuclear armaments, but would also eradicate the basis of the sort of thinking which contemplates their use. Only then could the *will* to disarm be permanently safeguarded.[6]

The consideration that democratic politics should be based on principles is far from being a new idea; in fact, it is coeval with democratic politics itself. Principled politics are a democratic tradition, and despite practices to the contrary, it remains a living one. Elsewhere, we have analysed the American Declaration of Independence as a model document for the application of principle.[7] Therefore it will suffice to mention here that the principles enumerated by the Declaration which all governments should safeguard, are the three 'inalienable' human rights: life, liberty and the pursuit of happiness. These principles are *formal* since they do not define any substantive goal the government must observe, nor do they suggest any concrete values, any forms of life that the government should promote. This is especially so in the case of the second principle, 'liberty', understood as negative liberty, for a government can only observe this principle if it does not intervene with the ways of life (in the broadest sense of the word) its citizens choose to engage in. At the same time, these principles are not entirely formal; they entail certain substantive considerations as well. This is true in particular of the principle of the 'pursuit of happiness' which is to be understood as a right to pursue *public* happiness, in other words, as the right to participate in all political decision-making processes.[8] What is even more important is the idea that the three political principles also serve as *moral maxims* for political action: those acting contrary to any of the principles infringe a *moral* norm. Of course, a democratic politician has to take responsibility for the consequences of his action of a type we have called 'Responsibility A', as he/she is 'in charge'. But his/her actions are not simply based on any calculation about 'good' or 'bad' consequences in an undefined sense; rather, it is in the observance or non-observance of principles that the consequences of political action can be said to be good or bad. Whatever the consequences, no political action in which the political actor fails to observe the three principles, is defensible. This implies the following conclusion: it is only those consequences which come about via the observance of the principles, the moral maxims of democratic politics, which can be deemed to be good. However, situations might emerge in which the observance of one principle collides with that of another (for example the collision between life and liberty, or negative and positive liberty). What are we supposed to do in such cases?

Whatever principles democratic actors may choose, the pursuit of public happiness (at least as a right, and eventually as an obligation as well) must, for obvious reasons, be one of them.

Democracy is by definition the rule of the people; its notion, therefore, includes positive political freedom. The fact that a democracy operates with institutions which not only permit but also ensure the participation of all citizens in policy-making processes is not a principle which can be accepted or rejected by democratic politics for it comprises the essence of democratic politics itself. If it comes to a genuine conflict between the principles of positive freedom and life, the mere presence of such a conflict signalizes that something is wrong with democracy. A freedom which is not worth being defended by a free people is a sham freedom. Choosing mere life as against freedom (the good life) is self-defeating for democracies. Of course, as we have suggested in our book on the peace issue, in the face of a nuclear Holocaust a conflict like this does not exist because where it is not only our lives but all real and possible lives which are destroyed, the prospect of any positive freedom (the good life) is destroyed simultaneously. The question is more complex if conflicts arise between positive and negative freedom. There is no general answer to the question of how these conflicts can be solved, the less so as all concrete single conflicts may be solved in a different manner. But when we recommend certain principles for democratic politics which can also serve as moral maxims, we submit a proposal which, if accepted, would provide a guideline to the solution of the conflicts between the principles of negative and positive freedom as well.

Every culture that accepts democratic principles for politics (and every political actor in it), should apply these principles to all other cultures. This recommendation includes an obligation: democratic principles should not only be observed within a democratic state, they should be applied to the relations of a democratic state with all other states as well. The political principles of democracy are moral maxims as well. A moral maxim is universally valid and cannot have a restricted application. If we take seriously the notion 'humankind', it must be true that the same principles apply to each and every member of the cluster 'humankind'. Since we have accepted democratic principles for politics, we ought to act such that these, and only these, principles should be accepted in each and every culture. This 'ought' implies the obligation that we ourselves act accordingly here and now.

We would recommend the following as principles constitutive of a democratic politics:

1 Act as if the personal liberty of each and every citizen and the independence of each and every nation depended on your action. This is the moral maxim and the political principle of *freedom*.
2 Act in accordance with all political rules, national and international laws whose infringement you would disapprove of even in the case of just one citizen (or one nation). This is the moral maxim and the political principle of (political) *justice*.
3 In all your political dealings assume that all men and women are capable of making political decisions. Therefore submit your proposals and plans to public discussion and act in accordance with the outcome of discussion. Co-operate in the decision-making process with everyone who is ready to co-operate with you. If you do not accept the maxim: *vox populi, vox Dei*, resign all your power positions, and embark on convincing others of the correctness of your opinion. This is the moral maxim and the political principle of (rational) *equality*.
4 Recognize all human needs, as long as their satisfaction is conceivable without collisions with the maxims of liberty, justice and (rational) equality. This is the moral maxim and the political principle of *fairness*.
5 In all your dealings support those classes, groups and nations which endure the harshest suffering, unless this postulate conflicts with the other maxims of political conduct. This is the political principle and the moral maxim of *equity*.

We recommend the acceptance of the above as the universal political principles of democratic politics. At the same time, they are moral maxims as they can act as guidelines for all moral decisions in any situation which includes or is related to, domination, power, force and violence. On the basis of these maxims we can also formulate the basic law of democratic politics:

Act in a way which allows all free and rational human beings to assent to the political principles of your action.

This basic law assumes the possibility of a *consensus omnium*, not a consensus in all political decisions but a consensus about the political principles of such decisions. If free and rational human beings assent to the principles of decisions and actions, this does not prevent them from querying, criticizing, or even opposing, particular decisions or actions of a body politic.

The first principle (the principle of freedom) does not distinguish between positive and negative freedom. It enjoins us to act such as to ensure the *personal* liberty of all actors (and the independence of all nations). Personal liberty (and independence) is thus, first and foremost, *negative freedom*. However, in its capacity as negative freedom, freedom is (in that it can be conceived as) the precondition of practising positive freedom. The third principle, that of *rational equality* regulates the application of personal freedom as *positive freedom*. It goes without saying that the equal and rational use of liberty is what positive freedom is all about. (Aristotle called it free equality or the equality of the free.) It is the fourth principle above that provides the guidelines for the solution of the eventual conflict between positive and negative liberty: the conflict has to be solved in a 'fair way'. But how can it be? Negative freedom (the pursuit of any of our needs, the pursuit of private happiness) ought to be guaranteed unless it collides with the personal liberty of others, with justice and with positive freedom. In this understanding, 'fairness' is not identical with justice, it is something *beyond justice*. Justice can only serve as a limiting factor of fairness in the event of a collision of the two, in which case justice *should* serve as a limiting factor for justice is superior to fairness, and so is positive freedom. If the pursuit of private happiness is not unjust, if it does not presuppose the use of other persons as mere means (which is an offence against the liberty of others), if it does not infringe the norm of rational equality (which is an offence against positive freedom), it has to be acknowledged and guaranteed in full. Put simply, neither the principle of justice, nor the principle of rational equality (positive freedom) applies to negative freedom, for an obvious reason. Human beings are unique, in this sense they are not equal, they cannot and must not be equalized as far as the pursuit of happiness (the satisfaction of their multifarious needs) is concerned. The inequality, or, more precisely the uniqueness, of human beings is intrinsic in the very idea of negative freedom. No principle applies to negative freedom except the principle of its recognition. Of course, people cannot subsist without observing at least one norm and, as a rule, they observe more than one. Observing norms-and-rules is Janus-faced. On the one hand, norms-and-rules set by the particular communities must not, either in isolation or together, contradict the political principles and moral maxims of democratic politics or else there is no longer any democratic body politic. On the other hand, negative freedom is only secured if these norms-and-rules, in isolation and together, are *not* substantively defined by any or all of these principles. In the practice of their negative freedom, men and women are free to *choose* norms-and-rules adequate to their needs, to their ways of the pursuit of private happiness. Here a reference to Nozick's Utopia is necessary. Utopia in Nozick, as we know, is the social condition under which all kinds of Utopias can be realized. While ensuring negative freedom (with the above proviso), democratic politics provide the framework for a variety of different forms of life, different kinds of the 'pursuit of happiness'. The principle of fairness enjoins us to act such that everyone who pursues his/her happiness in his/her own way has to recognize the right of everyone to do the same. The principle is observed if no other common rule applies.

The moral maxims of democratic politics are no different in the task they perform to that which any principle applied to any human culture is supposed to perform. Democratic principles are the universal standard norms-and-rules to which we can appeal without contradiction in each and every instance where actions are embedded in, or related to, domination, power, force and violation. The principles were formulated such that, if applied, they would minimize domination (within a state and in inter-state relations), exclude violence, minimize force and decentralize power. The fourth principle excludes the use of force and violence in *every* human interaction and secures the recognition of all norms, moralities, customs (ways of life) in whatever cultural context they may be embedded in, unless they include domination, force, power and violence. Finally, the fifth principle takes cognizance of the particular claim of human suffering. Those acting according to the principles of democratic politics are obliged to provide at least minimal conditions for the implementation of the same principles for everyone (every person and every culture). Hobbes made it clear that if the reproduction of *life* is not guaranteed, the Commonwealth relapses into 'the state of nature'. The principle of the 'recognition of all needs' is far broader than the recognition of the need for life (since the former implies the recognition of the need for the good life as well) but it clearly encompasses also the recognition of the need for life. Thus the fifth principle is a further specification of the fourth principle, and it enjoins us to ensure that all needs ought be equally recognized but that the needs of those suffering most have to have a *priority* in *satisfaction*.

A sceptical observer could charge at this point, that although these moral principles may sound all very well and good, they are unsuited to political practice of any kind. Political decisions have to be made, political judgements have to be passed here and now, and a self-abandonment to day-dreaming and wishful thinking is anything but a sound contribution to the daily labour of political actors. Both politics based on an 'ethic of responsibility' and on 'ultimate ends', some readers may argue, offer more tangible recipes for action than our fancy principles. If one follows in the footsteps of Kissinger's principles, one at least knows exactly what to do. If one is convinced that the nationalization of all 'means of production' and the establishment of 'the dictatorship of the proletariat' means the solution to all problems, one can act such that the desired results come about. But what can one *do* with the aforementioned principles in a world from which even the remote possibility of their consensual acceptance is absent?

However, these, and similar, objections seem to be too hasty. The consensual acceptance of the moral maxims of democratic politics is indeed a Utopia and as such, it is counter-factual. But this does not at all mean that the principles are 'not real' (in the sense of being regulative at least for some people), nor does it mean, more importantly, that they *cannot* be applied *anywhere*. It only means that at present they are *nowhere* applied *consistently*, and further, that, at present, they *cannot* be applied *everywhere* (in this sense, at present no full consensus can come about). We are convinced that these principles can be applied by the democratic left and that they *should* be applied. In our *judgement*, the principles can be applied without difficulties. The left can, and should, judge all political actors and systems from the vantage point of these same principles. No political actors observe these principles completely, but *some* do observe them to greater or lesser degrees. If the left compares and ranks different political actions and actors (whatever cultural context they might appear in), it can and should begin a process of comparison in accordance with the guidelines of those principles. In any particular political decision one can side with those who observe the principles more than other actors do, without thereby committing oneself to cease criticizing them in terms of the principles they do not observe. What is true about judgement is equally true about certain political actors. If two political actors (systems) are on a collision course, and one of them observes the principles to a greater degree than the other, the left should side, not only in judgement but in action, with the former, without relinquishing the right to criticize the inconsistency (in observing the principles) of the party it basically supports. And all movements and parties on the left should, when launching a programme, *test* it in one crucial respect: whether or not its objective, if it were to be realized successfully, would promote actions in accordance with the principles of democratic politics. It is in this sense that the moral maxims (political principles) of democratic politics can serve as regulative ideas both in our judgement and action here and now. If their acceptance as such is rejected as 'merely Utopian' there is no hope left for the radicalization of democracy.

Notes

1 For an analysis of all these problems see A. Heller, 'The moral maxims of democratic policies', in *The Power of Shame*, London: Routledge and Kegan Paul, 1983.

2 For Weber's discussion of politics and ethics, see 'Politics as a Vocation' in Gerth and Mills op. cit., especially p. 120 ff.

3 Lukács mentioned to us the contempt with which Weber had analysed repeatedly for him the devastating consequences of a politics conceived as a mere power game. 'This is why, after Bismarck, we never had a politician for a chancellor, and after Moltke – a genuine strategist for a general' – he said bitterly to Lukács.

4 It is not generally known that in his famous lecture 'Politics as a Vocation' Weber attacked his young friend Lukacs, then the most famous convert to communism, personally. Weber turned, with disappointment and perhaps with cold hatred against Lukacs. But all those familiar with fragments of Lukács's (planned but never completed) bool on Dostoevsky, in prepara-tion during the first months of World War One, with which Weber, of

course, was familiar, know that his allusions to the 'Dostoevskyan ethic' in 'Politics as a Vocation' are references to Lukács.

5   In reconstructing Kissinger's 'ethics of responsibility' we have relied, in the main, on his *White House Years*, Little and Brown, Boston, 1979, the theoretical premisses of which were already articulated in his Metternich book, *A World Restored: Metternich, Castlereagh and the problems of peace, 1812–22*, Weidenfeld and Nicolson, London, 1957. What we have called here the Brezhnev-doctrine was formulated as such in an outburst by Brezhnev during the August, 1968, 'negotiations' with the captured Czechoslovak leadership: '. . . your country lies on territory where the Soviet soldier trod in the Second World War. We bought that territory at the cost of enormous sacrifices, and we shall never leave it. *The borders of that area are our borders as well.*' (our italics) Z. Mlynár, *Night Frost in Prague*, C. Hurst and Co., London, 1980, p. 240.

6   We have elaborated our views on the peace issue in A. Heller and F. Fehér, *Doomsday or Deterrence*, Sharpe, New York, 1986.

7   A. Heller, 'The moral maxims of democratic politics', ibid.

8   This question is discussed in detail in H. Arendt' *On Revolution*, The Viking Press, New York, 1965.

6

Citizen Ethics and Civic Virtues

Morals can best be described as an individual's practical relationship to the norms and rules of proper conduct. Two aspects of this relationship can thus be distinguished: the individual's relationship on the one hand, and the norms and rules of proper conduct to which the individual relates himself or herself on the other. Using Heglian categories we would term the first aspect 'morality' and the second aspect *Sittlichkeit* (collective moral habits, norms and prescriptions). There are norms and rules of proper conduct in all fields of action, interaction, communication. Morality is therefore not a sphere to be distinguished from all other spheres, nor is it an institution one can distinguish from other institutions. No sphere or institution is purely moral in character. They all include certain norms and rules belonging to *Sittlichkeit*, that is, norms and rules the observance of which is regarded as good or right, the infringement of which is regarded as bad or wrong.

We can distinguish three typical spheres in all non-tribal societies: the sphere of everyday life, the sphere of economic and political institutions and the sphere of cultural ideas and practices. It is the latter that produces meaningful world-views, that renders meaning to life and lends legitimacy to the other two spheres. World-views can, incidentally, be used critically, namely as ideological devices to test and query the goodness and rightness of existing institutions and forms of life. In premodern times all spheres were imbued with the common norms of *Sittlichkeit*. Living in each sphere required more or less the same virtues. A constellation like this can be described as a 'dense ethos'. In modern times, spheres have been differentiated to a previously unknown degree. Economic and political institutions have parted ways, and the differentiation between public, private and intimate spheres has been actualized. All these spheres and their sub-spheres developed norms and rules of *Sittlichkeit* of their own. The division of the cultural sphere into independent sub-spheres both expressed and prompted this development. Science liberated itself from religious constraints and eventually became the dominant world-view of modernity. Simultaneously, art and philosophy have also emancipated themselves by rejecting the imposition of alien norms on their autonomous territory. All spheres of modern life thus developed their own intrinsic norms and rules of *Sittlichkeit*, though not always to the same degree. Yet there are so few norms actually shared by all of them that sceptical and pessimistic theorists could plausibly argue that spheres of life are both irreducible to one another and irreconcilable in terms of their value content. This, for instance, was Weber's standpoint. Nowadays we have no reason to be so sceptical. For example, we reject racism and sexism in all spheres and, at least theoretically, to an equal degree in each. This indicates that a kind of common ethos is still present or that it has presented itself once again. Yet this common ethos is not dense, for it does not query the autonomy, or the relative autonomy of the various spheres and sub-spheres of life. It only enjoins that the specific norms of the spheres and sub-spheres should not contradict the meta-norms of *Sittlichkeit*. We would term such an ethos a 'loose ethos'.

'Citizen ethics' are obviously related to the norms and rules of political action and to the meta-norms of the 'loose ethos'. Whether or not a person visits a friend in hospital, whether he/she is friendly or unfriendly, kind or unkind, generous or ungenerous, has no direct bearing on his/her being a good or bad citizen. These and similar virtues or the lack thereof are private matters. Furthermore, there is a great variety of forms of life in modern civil society, and each of them has a set of norms and rules of its own. If one chooses a form of life (or, at a later stage, chooses once again the one into which he/she was born), one, as it were, makes a promise, a commitment. Failure to live up to such a commitment represents an infringement of the *Sittlichkeit* of the particular way of life, but it does not necessarily mean that one has also infringed the norms and rules associated with being a good citizen. Finally, unless strong moral reasons dictate otherwise, observing the sphere-specific norms of non-political institutions is also a matter of decency yet even this has very little to do with being a good citizen. In drawing such distinctions, we have not sought to excuse those who shun the performance of compassionate deeds, those who fail to live up to their private promises or who perform their obligations badly, not even when they excuse themselves by referring to their commitment to urgent public duties. Our only aim has been to point out that 'citizen ethics' do not encompass ethics in its entirety.

II

Every adult member of a modern democratic state is by definition a citizen. But not everyone has an individual practical relation to the norms and rules of the political sphere and to any action or decision related to that sphere. In discussing 'citizen ethics', we refer to the norms and rules which attach to citizens who actively participate in the political sphere and not to nominal citizens. To say that a citizen stands in a 'practical relation' to the norms and rules of the political sphere also requires qualification. For example, a political scientist stands in relation to the political sphere, but this relation is theoretical rather than practical: he/she relates to this sphere as an observer, not as a participant. Needless to say, the same person can be both an observer and a participant and can switch from one attitude to the other and vice versa, but the two relations are still distinct. Furthermore, one can also be an actor, a participant member in spheres other than the political. For example, everyone without exception has an active relation to the sphere of everyday life.

One can practically relate to the political sphere without having chosen politics as a vocation. Since Weber was deeply concerned about the fateful consequences which would ensue from confusing the norms and rules of the separate spheres of life, from an intended or unintended encroachments by norms belonging to other spheres on the political, he insisted that politics required a certain vocational orientation. If the danger of 'conflating' different sphere-specific norms and rules can be prevented by vocational choice alone, citizen action would be narrowed down to that of vocational politicians or professional revolutionaries, and citizen ethics would be tantamount to vocational or professional ethics. However, there are no compelling reasons to accept this proposition which is detrimental to the democratic principles of politics. Whatever a person's profession or vocation, in whatever sphere he/she is active, all members of a democratic body politic can also relate practically to the political sphere. Indeed, it is important for every citizen to learn not to confuse sphere-specific norms and rules with one another. For example, the aestheticization of politics, seeking redemption in politics or applying the rules of science to political action, are all equally dangerous inclinations which need to be resisted. Routine actions which play such an important role in the sphere of everyday life, are far less warranted in the political sphere. Yet every citizen can learn, and indeed does learn, how to alter his/her attitude when entering the sphere of political action. Furthermore, the democratic principle of the citizen's active political participation is not to be supported by a defensive argument alone but also by an offensive argument. People who choose political action as a vocation, including so-called professional revolutionaries, are inclined to take the prevailing norms and rules of the political sphere for granted. People who switch to and fro between the political sphere and other spheres, can enliven a certain critical potential. Without imposing alien norms on the political sphere, they can still challenge the taken-for-granted character of one or another political rule, in particular, the justice, the viability and the rationality of certain institutions. The broader the life experience, the more multifarious the needs of political actors, the greater is the likelihood that just norms and rules might be substituted for existing ones.

It is not altogether easy to distinguish between social and political action. Whether the action is individual or collective in nature does not decide the matter. Nor does the concrete character of the very issue under deliberation or contestation. In a rough approximation, actions can be termed political if persons act in their capacity as citizens, and if they address, or incidentally mobilize, other persons in their capacity as citizens. This can happen in three distinct ways. Firstly, persons can act within political organizations, secondly, persons can translate private grievances into public issues and, thirdly, persons can handle, or mobilize others to handle, social or private issues by having recourse to general or universal political ideas, rights and democratic norms. These three types of political action can merge but they do not always do so. All three types of political action require civic virtues.

III

Virtues are character traits which are regarded as exemplary by a community of people. Such character traits are acquired by practice. To do right things and to do them in a right fashion indicates that a person desires to develop certain virtues in himself or herself, or at least to look as if this is what he/she wants to do. To do the right things in the right fashion consistently and continuously indicates that the persons in question have succeeded in acquiring exemplary character traits. The virtues (or exemplary character traits) are related to values. Values are goods. Anything can be a good – be it a thing, a social institution, a feeling, a human relation, a superhuman being, a state of mind, a kind of discourse, if a *worth* is attributed to it by a particular community. Pure values are meta-goods in so far as their presence or absence defines the worth or worthlessness of a particular thing, institution, human relation, state of mind and the like. Formally very similar character traits and practices can be regarded as virtuous or virtue-indifferent depending on whether or not they are related to a value. A person who risks his/her life for a cause is courageous. By contrast, a stuntman's daring is not a virtue but an excellence of a kind. Certain character traits may be considered virtuous by a community in one particular historical period whereas they can be viewed indifferently, even as vices, in another. Certain other virtues are frequently reinterpreted in conjunction with changing value orientations. Where hierarchy is a value, humility and blind obedience are virtues. Where equality is a value, they are no longer virtues, but vices. Certain virtues and vices are constant. Their constancy indicates that they are related to certain constant forms of human relations and associations which are always considered worthy. Generosity is generally regarded as a virtuous character trait, as is justice. Envy, vanity, rancour or flattery are generally regarded as vices.

It follows from the above that one cannot discuss civic virtues before discussing the values to which such virtues are related. Civic virtues are the citizen's virtues. The value to which they are related must be a thing, a social relation, a state of mind, a kind of discourse, a feeling or something else, but it must certainly be something which has an intrinsic worth for every citizen irrespective of their religious or lay creed, their individual aspirations, professional commitments, tastes and the like. Cicero said that civic virtues are related to the *res publica*, the republic, which literally means the 'common thing'. Contrary to Aristotle, he knew that we share something with the whole human race, namely reason. As a man of common sense, he also knew that we share far more with the members of our family than with our fellow citizens: we share practically everything with the people with whom we live under a common roof. The common thing shared by all citizens and by them alone is not the most general good (for this is shared by all humankind), nor is it the sum total of all goods (for these are shared by the members of the family or by close friends) but the goods regarded as the conditions of the good life. Institutions, that is, the laws of the republic determine whether we are able to conduct a good life at all.

Cicero's common-sense argument is certainly not an outmoded one. We can still say that there are certain goods we all *share* and that these goods are things of such intrinsic worth that we consider them to be the preconditions of the good life. Citizen virtues are related to such commonly shared goods of intrinsic worth.

What kinds of goods do *we* hold to be goods of such intrinsic worth, in other words, what kinds of values do *we* hold in common?

Naturally, no theorist can *invent* such values. A theorist only can pinpoint values which already guide the actions of certain people and which are accepted (regarded as valid) by others even if their actions are not guided by them. If actions are guided or informed by certain values, we can refer to such values as 'regulative'. If values are accepted as valid even if they do not inform action, we can term such values *fully counter-factual*. Of course, values are counter-factual also in their regulative use as long as the value in question is not embedded in institutions or social relationships, if they are not accepted by everyone, or perhaps even as long as they are not completely taken for granted. Values which are accepted by everyone and are already taken for granted, are termed 'constitutive'. The value of universal suffrage became a constitutive value in modern democratic states. If all international conflicts were to be settled by negotiation and discourse, and never by force, peace would become a constitutive value. Now at the very best, peace is a regulative value, though, by and large, it is a fully counter-factual one. For some, however, it holds no value at all. We mention only in passing that ultimate meta-values can never become constitutive even though they may function as levers which transform other values from their regulative status into constitutive values. Freedom as such, as an ultimate meta-value, cannot ever be, so to speak, 'realized', although different 'freedoms' can. It follows from all this that although theorists cannot invent values, they certainly can pinpoint counter-factual, even fully counter-factual, values. In what follows we should like to discuss certain commonly shared values and the civic virtues related to them in this spirit. If the question is raised as to whether our discussion is a factual or an evaluative one, whether we are placing a particular interpretation on a set of facts or arguing for certain norms, we can only answer by saying that we are doing *both*. We shall indeed argue for the validity of certain norms but we derive these norms from the real commitments of real people. The list of civic virtues we shall be proposing is normative though such civic virtues are factually practised, developed and approved of by real people in contemporary conflicts and situations.

What are the goods which we regard as the conditions for the good life for all? Which are the goods that have an intrinsic worth for all? We frequently ask these and similar questions and try to give answers to them. Although the answers to these questions will certainly have something to do with our problem, strictly speaking, there can be no definitive answers to them. This is so because *not all goods* regarded as the conditions for the good life for all or having an intrinsic worth for all, are things we 'commonly share'. Loving or being loved is, obviously, a condition of the good life for all and it indeed has an intrinsic worth, yet it is not a 'common thing'. Common things are constitutions, laws, public institutions, decision-making bodies, general (that is, commonly shared) frameworks within which social institutions, economic or other in character, operate. In addition, the set of procedures under which such bodies are established, which keep them going or allow them to be replaced by others, is something which is commonly shared. The publicly shared goods are 'ideal', that is, at the very best they secure the *socio-political* conditions for the good life of all, and not *all* the conditions of such a life. The socio-political conditions of the good life have traditionally been associated with *justice*. The 'common thing' which is good for all and is, at the same time, the condition for the good life of all, is justice or, to be more accurate, the common thing, the *res publica* is good for all if it embodies justice.

Citizens contest the justice or injustice of common institutions. Both when they attack the unjust or defend the just character of such institutions, they adopt the standpoint of a value other than the value of justice. This cannot be otherwise, for one cannot answer the question 'why is this institution unjust?' by replying 'because it is not just.' There are two values to which both the contestants and the contested normally have recourse in their attack or defence of social arrangements: the value of freedom and that of life. In modern times, both values have become universalized. Universalization opened up the possibility of a great variety of value interpretations. As long as values are concrete, there is little scope left for interpretation. For example, the value of 'national independence' is fairly unambiguous. There cannot be contradictory interpretations of 'national independence'; conflicts are more likely to emerge over the evaluated means of achieving or preserving it. Yet universal values permit contradictory, not only divergent, interpretations. That is both the contesting and the contested parties can have recourse to the same values, subjecting them to differing interpretations. Furthermore, meta-values can inform the evaluation of quite different institutions to which an intrinsic worth is to be attributed. However, if concrete values differ, the virtues related to such values will also be different in kind.

At this point we should like to raise a strongly normative claim which is not without empirical foundation. We accept the most universal interpretation of the universal values of freedom and life as the very value to which civic virtues are related. This interpretation can be summed up in the following way: 'equal freedom for all' and 'equal life-chances for all'. In this interpretation the universal values of freedom and life are combined with the conditional value of equality. Such an interpretation of universal values calls for the participation of everyone concerned in the establishment of the institutions of the 'common thing'. Finally, we accept the view of Habermas that rational discourse is the optimal (the best) procedure by which to attain the 'common thing' – only such a discourse can provide a procedurally just basis for the deliberation and contestation over competing values. Thus we would add a fourth value, that of communicative rationality, to the list of values which are to establish the intrinsic worth (goodness) of common institutions. Thus our two questions can be reformulated as follows: what are the civic virtues all citizens should excel in if they attribute an intrinsic worth to commonly shared institutions informed by the universal values of freedom and life, by the conditional value of equality and by the procedural value of communicative (discursive) rationality? The main civic virtues related to such values are the following: radical tolerance, civic courage, solidarity, justice, and the intellectual virtues of readiness to rational communication and *phronesis*. Let us briefly discuss each of these.

1   If one subscribes to the interpretation of the value of life as 'equal life-chances for all', one should recognize *all human needs*, with equal recognition granted to each, excepting those needs whose satisfaction requires by definition the use of other humans as mere means. Some examples of these are those needs which entail oppression, domination, violent and sadistic practices and the like. The latter needs have to be excluded from recognition because, were we to recognize them, we would be prevented from recognizing all concrete needs. The recognition of all human needs (excepting the afore-mentioned) is tantamount to the recognition of a great variety of forms of life. All

forms of life with the above proviso should be recognized as good and thus respected. This does not mean that forms of life cannot be cricitized: they can and must be criticized though criticisms can only be levelled if recognition is granted first. Criticism, combined with mutual recognition, accompanies the acceptance of the procedure of rational discourse conducted about values. We refer to the virtue of recognition of different ways of life and the readiness to enter into rational value-discourse with its adherents the virtue of 'radical tolerance'. Tolerance is a traditional value in liberalism and, as such, one of the preconditions of negative liberty which all democratic politics must preserve. But when applied to the coexistence of different ways of life, liberal tolerance simply means that I pursue my happiness in my own way, you do it in your own way, and the one is of no concern to the other. Recognition, however, carries a more profound and complex meaning: in it, other people's alternative ways of life are *our* concern even if we do not live them ourselves. 'Recognition' is therefore a *positive* category, an assertive one. It implies an active relation to the other without violating the other's negative freedom, the freedom from interference. Radical tolerance does not tolerate force, violence of domination. Those persons who have acquired the virtue of radical tolerance, will fight for the recognition of forms of life, and they will challenge laws as unjust in so far as they exclude such forms of life from recognition. Eliminating discriminatory laws against homosexuals is a case in point. Yet if confronted with ways of life embued with violence and domination, persons who hold to the virtue of radical tolerance will plead for legislation against such use of force: here rape in the family is a case in point. Both examples illustrate the fact that radical tolerance cannot be confined to the gesture: 'this is none of my business' but implies rather the gesture: 'I do care'.

2   Civic courage is the virtue of speaking up for a cause, for the victims of injustice, for an opinion we believe to be right even against overwhelming odds. The virtue of civic courage induces us to take risks: the risk of losing our safe position, our membership in political and social organisations, the risk of being isolated, of having public opinion against us. A person with civic courage does not court disaster, he/she does not seek confrontation for confrontation's sake. He/she acts out of democratic conviction, in the hope that justice can be done, that the dissenting opinion will be accepted by others, that the good cause is given a chance for victory. But even if this is not the case, the person of civic courage will stand his/her ground unless he/she is convinced by

others that he/she is in the wrong. Convincing a person of civic courage
is not an easy task because he/she will inevitably raise doubts about
whether it is merely convenience or fatigue that has led him or her to a
change of mind. Civic courage is a traditional democratic virtue and
examples of it abound in a good deal of modern literature and cinema.
Ibsen's Stockmann (from *The Enemy of the People*) is a man of civic
courage while Nora is the female paragon of the same virtue. Films like
The Man Who Came from the West, *The Man Who Shot Liberty
Valance* or *Twelve Angry Men* made a strong impact on the popular
imagination precisely because their protagonists were the exponents of
civic courage. In the first two movies, both westerns, two different
kinds of courage are counterposed: courage in using physical force (the
traditional virtue of courage) and courage in defending values
rationally even against overwhelming odds (civic courage). In *Twelve
Angry Men*, as in Ibsen's drama, it is not naked, physical force but the
more sublime force of prejudice that is challenged by civic courage.

The virtue of civic courage is of no less importance in collective
actions. Yet each and every participant in a collective action takes his/
her risk as an individual. Civic courage is the kind of courage needed in
movements which relinquish the use of force, where no martial virtues
are required, by they movements of passive resistance or of civil
disobedience.

3   The third civic virtue is *solidarity*. This is a traditional virtue of the
left, the only virtue which, over a century ago, took up a distinguished
position in the ranks of social democracy and generally in the working-
class movements. The virtue of solidarity comprised two different
kinds of solidarity. One of them referred to the solidarity as practised
within an in-group, be it a party, a movement or a class. The second
kind of solidarity, in a form which was felt rather than practised,
entailed a sympathy or empathy, even a brotherly feeling, extended to
all dominated classes and nations, and eventually to humankind as a
whole. Critics of this all-encompassing feelings of brotherliness have
pointed out, often with a degree of contempt, that it is but a cheap
substitute for radical goodness, and that those who embrace all
underdogs or the whole of humankind inevitably fail to help a single
human being in dire need of practical support. Critics of in-group
solidarity have pointed out that it can produce unintended, even
negative results. Practical in-group solidarity is a problematic virtue
for it can also be a vice. Both Fascists and Stalinists held group
solidarity in awe. In such an atmosphere, the more a person turned

against that virtue, the greater the person's merit. Yet even if we dismiss past historical experiences and glance at the present alone, we have to admit that neither of the two critical standpoints has completely lost its relevance. Many of us are ready to express solidarity with remote movements in remote countries without lifting a little finger in active solidarity in our own social context. Again, there are many people who suppress their own opinions and lend support to decisions they regard as unjust or unfair because of their allegiance to an in-group solidarity.

Obviously, the virtue of solidarity is in need of redefinition. One cannot redefine the virtue of solidarity to exclude possible conflicts between it and civic courage but one can still remove the main ambiguities which have so far been inherent in this traditional and distinguished civic virtue. The kind of solidarity we are looking for has to be attached to the same values as radical tolerance or civic courage. Like them, it has to be informed by the universal values of life and freedom, by the conditional value of equality and by the procedural value of communicative (discursive) rationality. The kind of solidarity we have in mind relates to the traditional value of solidarity just as radical tolerance relates to the traditional value of tolerance. Radical tolerance requires the recognition of all forms of life except the ones which by definition include domination, violence, force (in short, the use of other persons as mere means). Similarly, the virtue of solidarity implies a readiness to translate the feeling of brotherliness into acts of support for those groups, movements or other collectivities which are intent on *reducing* the level of violence, domination or force in political and social institutions. Obviously, solidarity can also be extended to those groups which use violent means but only if they do so in self-defence, and only if they show an explicit readiness to settle their conflicts by negotiation and discourse as soon as the opposing party is ready to listen to arguments. The virtue of solidarity thus defined, does not include *unqualified* support for the in-group (nor for that matter, any other group or movement); rather it *excludes* unqualified support. Furthermore, the above qualification *mediates* between the in-group and humankind as a whole for all groups and movements which decrease domination, force and violence expand the territory of freedom and life-chances not only for themselves but also for the human race. Marx once pleaded for solidarity with the proletariat because, he believed, the liberation of that class would bring about the liberation of humankind. The theoretical aspect of Marx's message can be rejected, yet the message itself can still be defended. Very few of us still hold to the view that a single social class is the bearer of human liberation. We always need to discover through the use of evaluative standards which class, group or movement it is which contributes to general human liberation. Yet solidarity is a civic virtue in so far as it is granted to such groups and movements. If such an evaluation does not precede the act of granting solidarity, the virtue of solidarity retains only its traditional and ambiguous qualities.

As mentioned, civic virtues are related to the political sphere but they are not practised exclusively in this sphere. This is quite obvious in the case of radical tolerance and civic courage but much less obvious in the case of solidarity. However, the virtue of solidarity should also be practised in face-to-face relations, in everyday life and in several other spheres. Practising the virtue of solidarity requires a gesture of active help. Whenever someone we are familiar with becomes the victim of domination, violence, force or injustice of any kind, we must lend our support to the cause of the victim with civic courage. Indeed, we must do even more: we have to stand by the victim with advice, and give the persecuted shelter against the persecutors in a gesture of solidarity. Those who fail to lend such support fall short of all that the virtue of solidarity implies. Solidarity is a virtue which pertains to the *quality of life* to the same extent as radical tolerance or civic courage are.

4   Justice is the oldest of all civic virtues and does not require any redefinition. Civic courage and solidarity can be vested in wrong causes and miss their target if they loose their relationship with justice. Before one stands up for someone or something with civic courage, before one solidarizes with causes and with persons, one first has to pass judgement and this judgement has to be just. Just judgement requires a combination of partiality and impartiality. A partiality for the values into which the virtue of justice is invested should not be suspended but rather reinforced. But partiality for persons, groups, institutions must sometimes be suspended. Personal feelings and vested interests must be relegated to the background. Preliminary judgements also must be suspended for they can otherwise easily harden into prejudices. Self-knowledge is also a condition of just judgement. In order to suspend vested interests, personal attachments or resentments, prejudices and the like, one must know, firstly, of what they consist. Just judgement must also be well-informed. One can dismiss opinions and justifications only after having given them a hearing.

5   *Phronesis* or prudence is also a traditional virtue which is mobilized in the application of norms. Before engaging in action, one has to find out what norm applies to a particular case and how the action can best be performed. *Phronesis*, that is, good judgement in action, is learned in practice and if learned well, it becomes a good character trait, that is to say, a virtue. Recently, certain theorists have called into question the relevance of *phronesis* in modern life. *Phronesis*, it is argued, is mobilized if a norm or rule has already been accepted as good and right, yet it is irrelevant to the process of norm-contestation which dominates modern life. It is undoubtedly true that *phronesis* is not the intellectual virtue which is mobilized in deliberation and contestation over norms. We cannot rely solely on prudence to determine whether a norm or rule is good or bad, right or wrong. Yet if in the process of deliberation or contestation certain norms and rules prove to be good, right, better or more right than others, we have to apply them in due course, and it is precisely in the process of application that we need the virtue of *phronesis*. This is especially important in political practice where we have to make political *decisions* all the time, sometimes with little or no time for deliberation. The intellectual virtue which enables someone to make good decisions cannot be completely replaced by another intellectual virtue which has gained prominence in the modern age.

6   The outstanding intellectual virtue of the good citizen in the modern age, is the virtue of participating in rational discourse, the virtue of being ready to participate in such a discourse. No one can determine for himself or herself *what* good or just norms or rules are, what just institutions are or may be, and no one is authorized to impose his/her particular views of these on others. The latter can only be achieved through the use of force, explicitly or at least implicitly. The explicit use of force implies dictatorship, the implicit use of force implies paternalism. Both dictatorship and paternalism contradict the universal values of freedom and life, the universal norms 'equal freedom for all' and 'equal life-chances for all', even if not to the same degree. To live up to these norms requires a just procedure. A procedure is just if everyone concerned with an institution, social arrangement, law and the like participates in a rational discourse concerning the *rightness* or *justice* of such institutions, arrangements and laws. The just procedure demands that everyone concerned should be *ready* to enter into a rational discourse. This readiness is not an innate quality, although it is based on the mobilization of certain

innate qualities as all virtues are. The virtue of being ready to enter a rational discourse is enhanced as with all other virtues through its practice. But the generalization of the practice of rational discourse already presupposes the *presence* of this virtue in a considerable number of the members of a body politic.

Let us now summarize the argument we have advanced here. If we agree that the 'common thing', the *res publica*, should consist of institutions, laws and social arrangements which are informed by the universal values of freedom and life, by the conditional value of equality and by the procedural value of communicative rationality, then we have to practise the civic virtues which are related to such values. We have to develop in ourselves the civic virtues of radical tolerance, civic courage, solidarity, justice and the intellectual virtues of *phronesis* and discursive rationality. The practice of such virtues makes the 'city' what it is meant to be: the sum total of its citizens. Whatever other virtues men and women develop in addition to these civic virtues, contributes to their own good life. Civic virtues contribute to the good life of all.

7

The Pariah and the Citizen
(On Arendt's Political Theory)

I

When *The Origins of Totalitarianism* was published, in an atmosphere of general acclaim critics failed to observe the truly astonishing structure of the work.[1] Instead of commencing her analysis with the usual sweeping generalizations, Arendt consumed the first quarter of the book with a painstakingly detailed chronicle of Jewish emancipation, and that of the unfolding of political antisemitism *in minutiae*. And yet, this idiosyncratic structure allows a deep insight into her most profound intentions. The story of totalitarianism starts with *the story of the pariah*, and therefore with the 'exception', with the 'politically anomalous' which is then used to explain the rest of society, rather than the other way round. In this book and elsewhere in Arendt's work, the concept of the 'pariah' is extended from the paradigm of the Jew to the colonial native and then to the endless millions of 'stateless persons' who provide a better clue for understanding the true nature of the nation state than the latter's solemn declarations of citizen rights, the slaves of the pre-Civil War period and their socially unemancipated progenies of the post-Civil War period in the United States. Arendt even argued that had the lunacies of certain Allied politicians with regard to a defeated Germany come to fruition, the whole German populace would have become the pariah of the comity of Europe.

Notwithstanding the more general application of the term, the Jew remains for Arendt the paradigmatic example of the pariah. Gerschon Scholem found this term offensive for he correctly understood the condescending tone of Weber's celebrated analysis of the Jewish pariah which was Arendt's principal source for her analysis. Weber's morphology of the pariah was presented with the appearance of impartiality though, of course, he had well and truly internalized Nietzsche's myth of the 'religion of resentment' attaching to the unsuccessful. Had she been familiar with this objection, Arendt would almost certainly have remained as unrepentant as she was when facing Scholem's remonstrances in the Eichmann case. Her theory was distinguished by a unique absence of sentimentality. Love and compassion had for her nothing to do with the understanding of the political solution of the lot of the pariah; indeed, such sentiments were viewed by her as unnecessary impediments to intellectual reflection. Basically, Arendt borrowed only one theoretical insight from Weber: *the absence of political community* in the long history of the Jewish pariah in the Diaspora with a concomitant lack of political self-consciousness and, until it was too late, a general disinterest in the political affairs of the environment in which they lived. Religious mysticism as pseudo-politics, for Arendt who relies on Scholem's pioneering analysis of the Sabbatai Zevi movement, is but a substitute activity arising only after the fiasco of the movement, a gesture which acts out miscarried political passions in Messianism. (It should be mentioned in parentheses, that Arendt paradoxically does not seem to be familiar with the catastrophe which had preceded, and which triggered, the Sabbatai Zevi movement whose classic portraitist is the great Yiddish writer, Singer. We have in mind the first Holocaust of the eastern Jewry suffered at the hands of Bogdan Khmelnitsky's *haidamaks*, an event which underscored the social and political conditions of the pariah's existence.) In Arendt's presentation, the Weberian pariah, the man of resentment appears as *a rebel* whose initially mystical aim, which gradually becomes a this-wordly strategy, is the transformation of the religious or ethnic community into a *people* or *a political community*, not necessarily in the framework of a nation state. If the pariah is a rebel, Arendt polemically argues against the mainstream of the Enlightenment, then its emancipation is not a 'social' one. A merely social emancipation gives rise to the *parvenu* who perforce pays with political excommunication for social glory, and with social excommunication for political ascendancy. Nor is genuine emancipation 'human', as Marx had contended in *On the Jewish Question*. For 'human' emancipation which, therefore, is neither social nor political, would only create a being without a political existence. Emancipation must be political and must establish thereby a political community, a people, though, to repeat, not necessarily in the form of a nation state.

Arendt identifies four paths allegedly leading to the emancipation of the pariah, all of which she regards as utterly misguided. These are: the 'organistic', the existentialist, that of 'emancipation through willing' and emancipation through the redemptive act. The *organistic* attempt at self-emancipation can be a solely *individual* act without further consequences, a sudden 'liberating movement' of internal self-illumination which has no impact on one's life strategy. This is the case when the assimilated Jew recognizes, during a testing period for the Jewish community, that there is 'something' in his/her emotional make-up which would render life unbearable, should the community to which he/she never belonged in any conscious way, perish. Alternatively, it can also arise in the form of a sudden collective experience of 'an innate affinity' the result of which is the emergence of a new nationalism. Such a result is seen to be of dubious merit by Arendt who critizes the mainstream of Zionism precisely on this score. The existentialist path is perhaps best exemplified by Sartre's well-known thesis, set forth in his preface to Fanon's *Wretched of the Earth*, in which the self-emancipation of the of the native is conceived in terms of a 'therapeutic' violence. Arendt clearly detested Sartre's politics of 'the radicalization of evil', his recommendation that the aboriginal should 'opt for himself' through destroying others, on the grounds that what commences as violence glorified *qua* 'self-therapy', will inevitably end in unfreedom. The third, and closely related scenario, sees the political pariah 'will himself or herself' *qua pariah* whereby the act of willing transforms the pariah's existence into freedom. Arendt quotes Lafayette's dictum: 'when a nation wills itself, it is already a nation', and terms it the last vestige of a *Christian politics* whose central category was precisely 'willing'. Her sharp eyes detect the remnants of a Christian politics in Rousseau's concept of 'the general will' which was to become allegorized, and, even more fatefully, institutionalized by Rousseau's greatest disciple in the cult of the Supreme Being. As far as a *redemptive* politics is concerned, both historical studies and philosophical inclinations sufficiently convinced Arendt that it is not an adequate response to the pariah's bondage but sham response and, moreover, a dangerous one which will eternalize bondage in the name of emancipation.

A conflict between the principles of *freedom* and *life* ensues inescapably from Arendt's understanding of the pariah's genuinely emancipatory political action. The conflict between these principles had a highly positive and an extremely problematic yield. If the pariah's cause is to be victorious everywhere, 'the human condition' in modernity must be that of a political freedom based on human rights, though not in any sense which implies the notion of a 'unified humankind'. But for this to happen, the Christian or pseudo-Christian 'politics of life', which is by the same token a politics of need and necessity, not that of freedom, has to be relegated to the background, otherwise we are bound for a global victory of the 'totalitarian syndrome' which means a *pariah existence for all.* This almost obsessive emphasis on freedom against life is no sign of hysteria. Arendt explicitly rejects the so-called 'Masada complex' and regards the calls for a heroic collective suicide as a symptom of political pathology. In addition, her emphasis on freedom, with which we fully concur, implies a far superior type of politics than the one prevailing in today's 'corporatist' societies. If we compare Arendt's passionate, though not at all theatrical plea for freedom and liberties, with Raymond Aron's sceptical understanding of a common 'human nature' allegedly underlying both western oligarchic pluralism and Soviet totalitarianism in the same degree and the same fashion, if we compare Arendt's theory with those projects whose pre-eminent value is *equality*, not freedom, and whose main concern is 'life', and thus the promotion of growth and the satisfaction of material needs, we certainly begin to see the uniqueness and superiority of Arendt's focus on freedom. Yet it is precisely this conflict between freedom and life which is the source of the problems which critics have pointed to in her separation of the 'social' from the 'political'. We shall return to this below.

II

Anyone familiar with Arendt's admiration for the ancient city-state will immediately understand that the following words from *The Human Condition* constitute more than a historical characterization; they chart a programme as well: 'In ancient feeling the privative trait of privacy, indicated in the word itself, was all-important; it meant literally a state of being deprived of something, and even of the highest and most human of man's capacities. A man who lived only a private life, who like the slave was not permitted to enter the public realm, or like the barbarian who had chosen not to establish such a realm, was not fully human'.[2] Our coming of age, our becoming human is coeval with the establishment of *the free institution of the republic*. Throughout her whole work, Arendt, an enemy of the theory of natural law, never ceased to emphasize that freedom (both in the sense of 'liberties', and 'freedom', or in that of 'negative' and 'positive' freedom), *is never 'natural'*. She critically contrasts the French tradition with its *Declaration* which speaks of 'man' *born* free, to the Greek and American tradition that asserts, the latter by its 'spirit' rather than in its fundamental texts, that we are born neither free nor unfree but we *create* and *establish* our freedom in and by the institution of the *republic*.

Arendt's central concept of 'the revolutionary tradition' and her abiding interest in it can only be understood in the light of this *non-natural*, created and re-created conception of freedom. Were freedom and liberties merely natural endowments of the human condition, it would be truly impossible to understand why revolutions break out, why freedom is re-created by them to the extent it is, and, even more, why they break out in particular periods. Of course, with Arendt there is no *causal explanation* of revolutions for freedom never has a 'sufficient cause' and it can never be fully deduced from any external event. Arendt unequivocally rejects both evolutionism and the Hegelian understanding of universal history as a process governed by the unfolding of historical 'laws'. These two negative and critical theses are the premises of her ambivalent campaign against Marx. Arendt's criticism of Marx is ambivalent in that she accuses Marx of abandoning the centrality of freedom through politicizing economics and by introducing the 'social problem', a substantive issue, into the problem of freedom which can only be an end in itself. This is, of course, a misguided accusation. Marx remained throughout the whole of his life a philosopher of freedom even to a degree which was already unacceptable for Arendt. He hated authorities of all kinds so much so that he wanted to abolish the state together with all Gods. On the other hand, Arendt rightly points to the particular feature which gives a deceptively smooth and very seductive explanatory power to the Marxian theory. Marx, the greatest of Hegelians, had firmly believed in evolution and the processional character of universal history with historical 'laws' as its indispensable accessories.

Arendt, an anti-Hegelian, adopts a less persuasive account of historical development and thus leaves a great many relevant questions open. And yet her conception of 'the revolutionary tradition' furnishes an important clue to the understanding of modernity which would be incomparably more convincing, had she combined, instead of rigidly separating and even contrasting, the 'social' and the 'political'. Revolution is in this theory a modern phenomenon *par excellence* the like of which was never known in earlier social and political turbulences. Revolution implies a 'new beginning' coupled with the publicly avowed aim of creating freedom, a self-conscious act of *foundation*. The revolutionary tradition has three branches. *The French Revolution*, the most spectacular episode within this tradition in fact introduced a most problematic, if now downright fateful 'pattern': the 'socialization' of the issue of political freedom whereby both social liberation (Arendt, of course, was extremely sceptical of this notion) and political freedom suffer a resounding defeat. In addition, the wrong tradition survived and attracted many followers and imitators. But even if it was not an outright proto-totalitarian system which grew out of this problematic branch of the tradition, at the very best, *democracy, and not a republic*, was the result. The *American* branch of the 'revolutionary tradition' was providential. As a result of the dedicated work of the American founding fathers, the most accomplished form of political freedom yet known was established in the American Revolution. However, for reasons which are inadequately dealt with by Arendt, the American example remained without followers. Moreover, the greatest of revolutionary promises, a republic which actualizes freedom at all levels of society and practises it day by day, was not realized in the American experiment either. Filling this gap could be expected of the third, as yet incomplete and, in a manner of speaking 'underground' branch of the 'revolutionary tradition': the often anonymous and collective struggles for *direct democracy*. The allegedly participatory system which reigned supreme in the Paris *sections* in 1793–4, the Paris Commune, the Russian Revolutionary Soviets of 1905 and 1917, and, finally, the Hungarian Revolution of 1956 whose historic greatness and wisdom Arendt never ceased to admire, were the main junctures in this long march which has not yet come to a halt and which is still awaiting its first providential opportunity for self-completion. However, once completed, this underground trend, misused and oppressed up until now both by revolutionaries and counter-revolutionaries, will give rise to the supreme form of a free republic.

Although more recently we have become accustomed to the idea of a 'republican tradition' – particularly in the wake of recent reinterpretations of Machiavelli, Arendt's sharp *contrast between democracy and republic* still remains remarkably insightful. This is particularly evident when we consider what this contrast does *not* imply. For instance, it has little to do with the technical meaning of the term 'democracy': for her, both the British monarchy and the French republic are democracies. Secondly, in distinguishing 'republic' from 'democracy', she is not concerned with the central problem of liberal theory: the dilemma of *positive* and *negative* freedom. For Arendt, any freedom which is purely negative, is perforce a mere transient phase of 'liberation' which must give way either to its establishment in a more positive form or to tyranny. Further, in her understanding, neither republic nor democracy should be interpreted in terms of the Tocquevillian reading of democracy in America (upon which, by contrast, Aron's whole theory rests), which has at its centre the key concept of 'equality'. Indeed, as far as the centrality of freedom is concerned, Arendt's republicanism is uncompromising, so that the differences which separate even a problematic pluralist system from totalitarianism cannot be reduced to mere differences in the degree of state-administrative immersion in society, as is the case, for instance, with Aron's theory. Finally, the alternative 'republic' or 'democracy' constitutes the exact obverse of Montesquieu's and Rousseau's well-known positions. The latter conferred an unambiguously positive value on 'democracy', and not on 'republic' but for both of them, and particularly for Rousseau, a democratic system seemed realizable only in a small and virtuous body politic.

What then are the features of *democracy* which account for Arendt's suspicion towards it? It means, firstly, the rule of consensus (or rather, one which leads, or at least tends, towards consensus) and for Arendt such a goal is inevitably tyrannical. Far from being consensual, opinions are irreducibly pluralistic, and *all opinions should be given a voice* in a free political community. Furthermore, a consensus can only be brought about by *majority rule*, an oppressive principle which is not to be confused with the simple technical device of all free political procedures in a limited time: *majority decision*. Majority *rule* means the *oppression of minorities*, either in the form of a systematic *social* discrimination, or the *political* silencing of the dissenting minority. Thirdly, consensus can only be achieved through, and result in, a *homogeneous will*, the ominous Rousseauean-Robespierrean *une volonte une* which transforms the free political process into a system of tyranny and organized witchhunts. Fourthly, democracy rests on *popular sovereignty*, an ingenious but highly questionable French institution. In Arendt's extremely debatable understanding of the American system, which, till this day, remains the closest to her republican ideal, the concept of 'popular sovereignty' was never an issue for the simple reason that in America there had been no sovereign prior to the constitution, only an internally free political community in the colonies. By contrast, in France, the new political system constituted around the key concepts *people* and *nation* was so devised as to replace the existing absolute sovereign and thus imported irresolvable complications into newly constituted French political life. Despite the fact that the term 'sovereignty' is indeed absent from the documents drawn by the American founding fathers, this statement is false on two counts. There had of course been a sovereign in the colonies against which the new American body politic was devised, namely the British. Further, the idea of the sovereignty of the people is a safeguard not just against kings, but also against a potentially oppressive government by the people's own elected representatives. Therefore, the principle of popular sovereignty is applicable to the American political system as well. Furthermore, the actual or potential 'corruption of the republic', as a danger, is acutely present in Arendt's own theory. She does not deny that even the best conceived republic, the American (let alone 'mere democracies') has degenerated into an oligarchy of a kind in which the so-called 'political elite' rules and the 'people' practise their freedom on the day of periodic elections only. As a result, *government* has been transformed into *administration* which is termed by Arendt 'the rule of nobody' because of the anonymity of decisions and the lack of personal responsibility. But if this is so, the concept 'popular sovereignty' retains its cogency and relevance and serves as a point of departure for all those who remain critical of the present state of affairs.

The final feature of a democracy which Arendt feels uncomfortable with concerns the character of *power* which she claims is fundamentally different in a 'democracy' than in a 'republic'. In the former, it is identical with the *state monopoly of violence*, a Weberian conception resolutely rejected by Arendt who points out the more than strange coincidence between Weber's and Trotsky's views on this matter. In the latter case power means *participation*. The different conceptions of power can perhaps best be illustrated by the particular theories of the 'social contract' and consent which underlie each of them. Disregarding the idea of a covenant, a particular type of 'contract' which, in Arendt's view, is only appropriate to a theocracy, there are two distinct versions of the 'social contract' and 'consent' theories. In the first version, the social contract is concluded between individual persons; it is based on reciprocal agreements (promises) and equality and it establishes a 'society' in the Roman sense of *societas* (that is, community or association). This version of the contract knows no distinction between rulers and ruled, and the consent which it requires is explicit, voluntary and conditional. The second version holds that a contract is always concluded between a population and its 'given' (pre-existing) rules and that the contract establishes a legitimate government. Consent here is mainly tacit, and therefore freely interpretable by the rulers. For Arendt, the first type pertains to the republic (including the American model), the second to democracy. She further adds that if even that part of the contract theory which is usually and correctly regarded as a myth, namely the legendary initial act of foundation of a *societas* is, in the case of the United States, a historical reality. Finally, the *foundation*, 'the first historical act', always has a more than symbolic significance for the republic. The fundamental principles of 'the republic' gain their enduring validity from the act of foundation. And the enduring quality (of traditions, institutions laws) is for Arendt one of the distinctive features of the republic, in sharp contrast to the reckless spirit of perpetual change so characteristic of democracy, with its unceasing metamorphoses of all laws and principles following an everchanging 'popular will'. This conclusion lends a certain conservative touch to Arendt's basically radical theory of the republic. It reformulates, without being able to answer, Jefferson's initial dilemma. Jefferson had asked, does a free people not possess the freedom to revise its own constitutive principles whenever it so wishes? But, on the other hand, would constant revision not lead to a self-inflicted devaluation of those same constitutive principles?

It should by now be sufficiently clear that the dichotomy 'democracy–republic' does not denote in Arendt two different sets of existing or 'desirable' institutions. Rather, the republic serves for her as a Kantian regulative theoretical idea of the free commonwealth of which modern democracy is but a very imperfect realization. However, regulative theoretical ideas, even if by definition they can never be 'realized', must descend from the heaven of theory to the earth of our political struggles. The actor in whom this descent is embodied and by whom it is realized, is the *citizen*. Arendt, a passionate and often biased critic of Marx, retains the Marxian dichotomy of 'citizen versus bourgeois' in full. She regards the victory of the bourgeois (the competitive private person) over the citizen as the single major catastrophe that befell Political Man and Woman in the nineteenth century. Indeed, this catastrophic victory set the scene for the triumph of the 'totalitarian syndrome'.

III

The distinction between the 'social' and the 'political' has a very precise significance in Arendt's theory. It can be found throughout her work but it comes into sharpest relief in *The Human Condition*. In the ancient world, the social was identical with the world of *needs*. Its proper location was the *household*, and its greatest theorist, the classic author of a *non-political* economy, was Aristotle. The world of needs, located in the household, is a *pre-political world*. Whoever is compelled by the misfortune of birth or external circumstances to dwell in it eternally, is a *pariah, not a citizen*, and therefore not fully human. For the prospective citizen, a mastering of the problems posed by needs is a *precondition* to becoming political, that is, fully human. The *social* therefore, *merges indistinguishably with the private*, or, more precisely, their separation had yet to come about. The dubious progress of the modern age was *the local and temporal separation of the 'social'*, the world of needs, from its initial and appropriate realm, *the private*, through the modern combination of technological innovation and the division of labour. This 'progress' resulted in the transformation of a hitherto household concern into a general issue for 'society', and, finally, as a result of these changes, in the 'socialization of politics'. By the latter Arendt means politics of the type whose major, and increasingly exclusive concern is no longer the issue of free self-government, an end in itself, but the 'social problem'. In other words, the elevation of *economic issues* onto the agenda of a given body politic. The new science arising from this change is *political economy* whose greatest philosophical exponent remains Marx. Marx did not invent the centrality of the social for the political when he raised productive capacity to the pinnacle of the human 'species essence' and made the principle of political freedom, which must be an end in itself, dangerously substantive. Rather, he simply expressed, with the unerring insight of his philosophical genius, the shifts that had taken place in modernity between the social and political, and drew the conclusions which they implied. Alongside this transformation there occurred a change in the conception of 'property'. *Property*, Arendt contends, is initially and primarily *not* associated with wealth. At least in ancient Greece, property was a correlate of participation: ownership of one's house conferred the right to participate in the political life of the city. Wealth became synonymous with property only in modernity, with the advent of the cult of *production* and *growth*. A 'socialized politics' operates with the Hegelian dichotomy of state and civil society which Arendt implicitly, but resolutely rejects as the false eternalization of a situation which greatly inhibits free political activity.

These dubious advancements of the modern age were finally solidified into the *liberticide political tradition in the French Revolution*. The Jacobins stimulated by the Rousseauean attitude of 'compassion for misery', translated the 'social question' into the language of politics. They abandoned the cause for freedom, the task of creating free institutions for the sake of resolving the 'social question', a question which is irresolvable through any revolution, instead of relegating it into its proper domain, the household. (The latter part of the statement strikes us as truly absurd especially in the light of Arendt's own theory which regards socialized production, consumption and distribution, which replaces household economy, as the distinctive feature of modernity.) Then and there, the 'totalitarian syndrome' was born. The Russian revolutionaries, more fascinated by the French political theatre on the stage of which misery became the sole spectacle and the exclusive political issue than by Marx's texts, learned their fundamental, and fateful, lessons from Rousseau's disciples. And even when politics are not degraded to a level of totalitarianism, they still remain, in modern times, captive to the primacy of the 'social realm'. For Arendt, the welfare state is therefore a contradiction in terms.

Before we embark on a criticism of Arendt's theory of the 'social' and the 'political', a distinction which strikes many of her readers at first glance as elitist arrogance, the following should be noted. The rejection of the relevance of the social for the political, which at times relegates the former to the level of household, while at others it leaves the whole problem simply unresolved, does not stem in Arendt from any sympathy she held for capitalism. Capitalism, for her, means above all *expropriation*, a violent act in which peasant masses were deprived of their property and freedom. Secondly, capitalism implies by its very existence and its expansive nature, *colonial imperialism*. And colonialism was the terrain where racism and the proto-totalitarian methods of government had first been tested. Further, she holds a very sceptical view of the free market, a phenomenon which, she argues, was an unmixed blessing only in the United States. At any rate, she rejects all types of politics which homogenize their sphere of influence under the common denominator of the free market and then call it a 'free world'. Finally, Arendt is an explicit critic of the cult of growth and its governing universe of competition. She regards the theory and practice of boundless growth as perilous to the human–

nature relationship, and she lauds the kibbutz, a collective way of life otherwise so alien to her own private nature, for fostering a new type of non-competitive human relations.

There are two typical ways of criticizing Arendt's separation of the private, social and public. The first is the way of the dogmatic liberal. The dogmatic liberal believes that the trichotomy is false in that it does not correspond to any reality and that it is potentially totalitarian. There is a public-political domain, that of the state or government with its external and internal concerns: diplomacy, warfare, law enforcement and minimum amount of organized charity. The economic sphere proper should ideally remain private without any collective or state interference. In this sense, the 'social', excepting social legislation is, or should be, private; that is, free individual enterprise. Since Karl Polanyi we have known that this idyllic view of modern economic and social affairs derives from nothing more than the myth of the self-regulating market. In no period of modernity was 'the social' (in the sense of the economic, though not exclusively the economic) abandoned to its own, allegedly self-regulating dynamic. It was constantly controlled, checked, deflected and supervised both by the state and public opinion.

The other type of criticism is radical and it is well exemplified by a recent paper by Richard Bernstein. Bernstein asserts that the trichotomy should be reduced to a dichotomy of the private and the political. Inserting the third 'realm' of the 'social' is methodologically misleading and politically dangerous. Not all questions *are* political, Bernstein admits, for this would indeed be totalitarian. But all questions *can become* political. His example, the problem submitted for Arendt's consideration by her critics at a conference several years ago, is housing. Arendt declared the problem to 'social' in that there is nowadays a consensus that 'everyone should have decent housing conditions'. However, as Bernstein pertinently remarks, the problem is *not* whether there is a public agreement on the abstract principles governing housing. Rather, the problem is to be located in the ways in which this agreement can be translated into practical results and since these are publicly debated, the whole matter *becomes political. Quod erat demonstrandum*: there can be no 'social' issue in Arendt's use of the term. However, Bernstein's own argumentation undercuts his own desire to reduce the trichotomy to a dichotomy and unwittingly lends weight to Arendt's conception, in a modified version. If there are matters which *are not* actually, but which *can only become* political (which are therefore *potentially* political matters), then the 'social' is non-existent *only if* the 'potentially political matters' *are exclusively private*. Yet, in Bernstein's own example these matters have already lost their exclusively private character in modernity for *general (in this sense: social) principles* are applied to them even in their private existence, i.e. when they are not publicly debated as political matters. The abstract principles: 'everybody should have decent housing conditions' indicates that in modernity, in stark contrast to the ancient world, certain public and general principles are related to many (but certainly not all) private affairs *even when these affairs are not raised* to a level of private–public debate. This 'no longer entirely private' and 'not yet, or not for the time being, fully political' but rather 'only potentially political' constitutes what Arendt, in our view properly, calls the 'social domain'.

In what follows, we shall attempt a redeeming critique of Arendt's trichotomy. The demand to return to the dichotomy from the trichotomy in *Arendt's sense*, by relegating the socio-economic to the realm of household, is an impossibility under modern conditions, further, it is outright reactionary if directly translated into the language of politics, and it would be suicidal for the central protagonist of Arendt's own political theory, the citizen. In her highly original 'parallel biographies' of the American and French Revolutions, Arendt locates the gradual paralysis of direct-participatory democracy in America in the *spatial* organization of cities, for instance, in the space of the townhall which was insufficient to admit all citiziens. And 'limited space' later became the architectural style of the townhalls mirroring *and* intensifying the principle of 'limited number'. However, she fails to grasp the incomparably more important *temporal* factors emerging in the French Revolution: the insufficient free time of the working citizens to participate in the *assemblée en permanence*, a problem brilliantly grasped, and phantasmagorically solved by Danton. In a modern body politic, namely one in which the majority of participants spend most of their time at work and in which at the same time, everyone is in principle a citizen, the 'social problem' cannot, in order to safeguard the political, be relegated to the private realm. Its solution has a *universal* significance.

Bearing in mind this important consideration which is rooted in the very dynamics of modern, differentiated societies, Arendt's trichotomy could, and in our view should, be 'redeemed'. Against Marx, she argued strongly that the political realm, which is not simply identical with 'the state', must neither be 'abolished' nor should it 'wither away'. It must be maintained, and it must have primacy. If political action is either totally 'substantivized' (i.e. totally reduced to achieving certain economic targets) or, even more so, if political freedom is sacrificed or even 'suspended' in the name of 'promoting growth' and 'alleviating misery', we relapse into a totalitarianism which would certainly deprive us of our freedom and which, moreoever, will not necessarily eliminate poverty. Arendt's provocative statement that revolutions can never solve the social question conveys precisely this message. In the republic, the 'social domain' will remain *a relatively separate aggregate of actions* (dealing with economic management, communal charity, culture, training and education) to which general and previously agreed principles apply. Here, they would be confined to their own 'realm', and would not aim at an overall change of the strategies of the body politic. If any of these practices of the social realm began to express a general wish for *strategic* change, then we shall have already proceeded from the 'social' to the 'political'. Until then, we remain within the domain of the 'potentially political', that is, the social. There is, furthermore, a very good reason for this separation. Given that economic, cultural, educational, etc. practices – in short, social issues – also constitute *ways of life*, frequent changes an inevitable result of politicizing social issues, would prove thoroughly disruptive for the body politic as well. The person who lives in a state of constant change or 'permanent revolution' is either violent or hysterical. But, given the constraints of time in the making of practical decisions in modern life, how is it possible to draw a clear line of division between a 'social' and a 'political' action? The answer is that it is often impossible. And yet, this unclear separation of the two domains causes problems only if we regard them as 'separate realms' or spheres. However, if we depart from the various 'capacities' of the social actor, as Agnes Heller has argued in 'The great republic', and not from unambiguously separable realms or spheres, the gravity of the problems is alleviated.[3]

Revolutions, these 'new beginnings', certainly cannot solve the 'social question', particularly not the problem of poverty, but the actors of free institutions, the citizens of 'the republic' can and should attempt to do so, if only in a provisional, rather than in any final sense. Arendt's thesis applies here as well: there is no 'end of history' in the 'social realm' either. And yet the citizen should act to solve the social question for three reasons. It is a *scandal for liberty* to tolerate misery in the given cultural understanding of the word, and even more in its strictly biological sense. Moreover, the perpetuation of poverty can only lead to the *suicide of liberty*: from mass poverty, only elites and mobs can emerge, not free actors. This was perfectly well known to the economic authority who is Arendt's source: Aristotle. Relative equality of wealth was for Aristotle a precondition of liberty. Finally, to divide the world into acts pertaining to freedom while rejecting the all too material demands of needs, and into other acts which satisfy needs and hence which pertain only to the realm of necessity, is a *false spiritualization of liberty*.

IV

'The politics of mortals', a term not explicitly used by Arendt but almost palpably implicit in her text (to my knowledge, the term was first used by Reiner Schürmann in relation to Heidegger), departs from the most banal 'fact' of the human condition: we are all mortals, and we are acutely aware of our limitedness in all our doings. This awareness triggers a sometimes concealed, sometimes overt, need to transcend our limitation. Both ancient and Christian humanity had open to them spheres and types of action in which this transcendence could be achieved. The first in pure contemplation, the second in devotion. As long as they remained 'uncorrupted', both were ends in themselves, and not meant to achieve something else. Nor were they mere palliatives. But such transcendences are no longer at our disposal. The first underwent, perhaps not irretrievably, a metamorphosis in which it became a mere quest for knowledge, the second was reduced to convention and a healing rite, in all probability irretrievably. *Only politics as an end in itself*, free public activity in 'the republic' remained for modern man and woman to immortalize the otherwise 'limited enterprise' of their lives. With an unexpected tenderness, Arendt dwells at length over the correspondence between the old Jefferson and John Adams where the former playfully experiments with the idea of a hereafter where he would simply continue his this-wordly business 'sitting in Congress with his friends and colleagues'. Jefferson's dream is the non-elitist dream of modern man and woman about immortalizing themselves in the politics of freedom as an end in itself. This is what 'politics of mortals' is all about. And even if in the foregoing we have tried to relativize the 'end-in-itself' character of political action, in the main, we would side with Arendt.

The first characteristic of 'the politics of mortals' in Arendt's theory is the rejection of the concept 'the end of history', the eschatological foundation of all 'redemptive politics'. 'The end of history', irrespective of whether it appears in an 'idealist', or 'materialist' version, involves the myth of an integrated process with its corresponding 'laws'. It promises an earthly paradise which invariably turns out to be a 'garden of fools', a period of deep disillusionment and cynicism. Belief in the 'end of history' renders our claims exaggerated, our promises irresponsible, our gestures intemperate, our convictions fanatical. The result is politics of a kind which promise redeemers and delivers us to inquisitors.

'The politics of mortals' also has an *anthropological* dimension. We have to learn to differentiate between the lust for *glory* and *success* and striving for *distinction* respectively. Lust for glory is the typical motivation of the feudal-Christian era and its correlative vices are vanity and haughtiness. Seeking success is the typical motivation of 'mass society' and its correlated vices and malaises are envy and frustration. Both are *monological* passions which do not placate the torments of our 'limited enterprise' but rather intensify them. However, striving for distinction is different in that it is *dialogical*. In striving for distinction, I distinguish myself from others through my deeds, I establish myself as a distinct 'I'. Should the process stop here, I would remain merely 'vainglorious'. But to be distinguished also means *to be recognized as such by others*, and not just, not even primarily, by signs of prestige and social hierarchy but, above all, by *confidence and trust*. And the latter only attach to acts of freedom. Jefferson, Arendt's favourite hero, was a man of distinction precisely in this sense, while the 'incorruptible' Robespierre was merely 'vainglorious'.

The third aspect of 'the politics of mortals' comprises a warning. Our posterity lives in our present deeds. We cannot transcend 'the future of the present', and therefore we *must not* attempt such a transcendence. Sacrifices are made by mortals in 'faith', this counterpoint to 'belief', and they are rational even if they reach beyond our limitedness by the very act of sacrifice. But since they are rational, they can only be made on behalf of the freedom of past and present mortals, the former given to us in tradition, the latter directly. To sacrifice present generations for the alleged freedom, and even more for an assumed 'well-being' of non-existing future mortals is the instrumentalization of the present, a blatant act of unfreedom. There is only one political act which hypothetically transcends our mortality, which endows our 'limited enterprise' with immortality, and this is the creation of *enduring and free* institutions.

However, a final feature of 'the politics of mortals' as the politics of freedom is not only missing from Arendt's conception but is explicitly rejected by her as unworthy of human dignity. This is the concept 'progress' which is, in our view, in a qualified sense indispensable for Arendt's own project. Progress can be understood as cumulative continuum or as 'gains without losses'. If it is given the first meaning, we have indeed returned to the irresolvable aporias of the Hegelian 'process' and 'the end of history'. If given the second meaning, progress is above all equivalent to what Arendt herself discovered in the American tradition. With a new realm of freedom, the pariah will be raised and the privileged reduced, to the level of the citizen which is the level of freedom. And irrespective of whether raised or reduced to this level, freedom can only be, by definition, a gain, never a loss. So understood, progress is both possible and indispensable.

Notes

1 H. Arendt, *The Origins of Totalitarianism*, Meridian, New York, 1958.
2 H. Arendt, *The Human Condition*, University of Chicago Press, Chicago, 1958, p. 38.
3 F. Fehér and A. Heller, *Eastern Left, Western Left: Totalitarianism, freedom and democracy*, Polity Press, Cambridge, 1986.

8

Against the Metaphysics of the Social Question

I

It was during the most radical phase of the French Revolution, that is, in the period of the Jacobin dictatorship, that 'the social question', and thus 'socialism' as a movement and the posited goal of History, were created.[1] Certain immediate objections to this position are of course predictable. Had not poverty existed prior to the French Revolution? Indeed, was it not an almost eternal feature of recorded history that the poor rebelled against the rich? Was democracy, as the rule of *demos*, not in fact aiming at the prosperous as the main target group in ancient Athens, occasionally in Rome, as well as in the renaissance republics? Cannot economic motivation be found behind the facade of religious and political ideologies in all major outcries and revolts? These legitimate questions will inevitably be posed against a thesis that derives the social question from the French Revolution, this watershed of modernity.

However, the term 'the social question', as it is commonly used in political parlance, both on the right and the left in modernity, is simply not identical to the brute, and thus far eternal, fact of poverty. Nor is it tantamount to political attempts at depriving the rich of their wealth, nor to 'economic motivation of political acts'. Rather, quite specific conditions of modernity have to be met in order for 'the social question' to be placed on the political agenda.[2]

Poverty, hunger, physical suffering without therapy or treatment, old age or childhood spent in indigence, orphans or dependents without providers and other millenial miseries of life could be summed up together by the common term 'the social question' only when the following conditions have been met: a society of estates, in which poverty and wealth were 'naturally' allotted to respective estates, had to be abolished in order for this conceptual change to take place. In addition, state and society also had to be, at least relatively, separated. Once this great emancipatory deed of anti-absolutist revolutions had been achieved, the dynamic of modern society was permanently characterized by a tense fluctuation between two extremes. One of these extremes has been the free-wheeling market, an allegedly automatic producer of abundance once it is left to its own devices. The other extreme is state intervention, which serves to protect the individual from the dark sides of this economic automatism. Ideological humanism of a kind also had to become a major spiritual power, making 'the right to life' not only an accepted maxim but also an operative political principle. It was not an accident that Robespierre was the first statesman who gave a pragmatic twist to the age-honored liberal demand for 'the right to life'. A socially accepted minimum level of the standard of life had to be defined, together with the emergence of a public view which could agree that if a considerable number of the citizens of the nation state should subsist below this level, then the situation should be regarded as an anomaly. This awareness of the socially anomalous implies the existence of a public, and constantly expendable, list of 'social issues'. These social issues in principle, although not necessarily in practice, require, indeed even demand, collective attention and attempts at their solution. All sorts of miseries, particularly poverty, had to be regarded as curable ills and not the eternal companions of human existence. This perception of human miseries as socially conditioned and therefore eliminable is a fundamental constituent of 'the social question' itself. The extreme ways which have been used to attempt to grapple with the syndrome also belong to this complex picture. One of these extremes is the recurrent attempt of liberal conservatism to return to a pre-revolutionary position, by declaring the whole, or parts, of the social question as an ontological constant of human existence and thus beyond human reach. Another extreme is a leftist radicalism of a kind which would destroy fundamental institutions of modernity (the market in the first place) and would thus inadmissibly reduce the complexity of modernity.

The first distinctive feature of 'the social question' consists of its thorough heterogeneity. In fact, practically the only common element amidst the paraphernalia of conspicuously diverse issues is the appeal of various social actors to the state, the demand or petition being to solve their particular social issue. Appeals of this kind imply a radical change of attitude. Since it is no longer the local community or the Church that seem to be the appropriate loci of problem-solving for modern men and women, charity has therefore been replaced by social legislation, the goal and task of which is redistribution. Thus, social issues have ceased to be moral in nature; they have been transformed into matters of social justice. The irreducible plurality and, by implication, unstoppable growth of the number of issues which have been declared 'social' have added enormously to the burdens of modernity. This plurality and irresistible growth of issues have contributed just as powerfully to making modernity a 'dissatisfied society' as has the apparently equally irresistible dynamic of need-formation.

Asserting that the French Revolution was the birthplace of the 'social question' implies two further statements, both of which have appeared in a programmatic context in modern politics. The first implication is the ultra-radical hypothesis that *the* social question as such can only be solved by *the* revolution as such. Two equally inadmissible, because too abstract, generalizations underlie this hypothesis. The first generalization asserts that the myriad social issues, which are by nature heterogeneous, can somehow be reduced to the homogenous formula of 'the social question', which is one and indivisible, and to which therefore a single and effective political remedy can apply. The second generalization holds that this remedy should be 'the revolution as such', whereby the heterogeneity of revolutions are similarly reduced to a homogenous formula. The second implication is the celebrated, or ominous, contrast between freedom and 'public happiness', the assumption being that by sacrificing the first, if only temporarily, the second could be promoted. However poisonous, the second implication was the permanent, sometimes overt, sometimes covert, premiss of what we have termed 'the metaphysics of the social question'.

II

Was Marx somehow personally responsible for the emergence of the metaphysics of the social question, as Hannah Arendt has suggested? In fact, if we cast an unbiased glance at the corpus of the writings of the 'founding fathers', we will find a surprisingly sparse interest on their part in 'the social question'. True enough, Engels wrote one of the most influential popular books on the poverty of the working class in his youth, a pamphlet which was widely read by conservative romantic anti-capitalist writers, who used it in their crusade against modernization. It is equally true that Marx quoted extensively in the first volume of *Capital* from the reports of English factory commissioners who were genuinely involved in fathoming the depths of the exploitation of the children's labour force. But as far as the bulk of their *oeuvre* is concerned, one would be genuinely surprised to what degree Marx and Engels remained unaffected by the fate of the class whose suffering they utilized for their bold philosophical conception. And as far as Georg Lukács, arguably the only philosophical genius of Marxism after Marx, was concerned, the social question simply did not exist.

Given these considerations, it would be a complete misreading of Marx's lifelong concern with alienation to understand it as an involvement in social issues.[3] The alienation of labour was not a 'social issue' for Marx, nor were its remedies, the simultaneous abolition of market, social classes and the state, recipes for curing social ills. The illness and remedy were together part and parcel of a radical anthropological project. The telos of this conception was the philosophical constitution of a homogenous and rational, but above all free and self-creative, humanity. Marx simply could not be concerned with the social question in terms of his own theory. In their present formation, it appeared to him to be a petty issue which deflected the proletariat from fulfilling its only adequate historical task, the creation of a revolutionary class consciousness, from becoming a 'class for itself'. Marx never ceased to emphasize that exploitation is not an issue of higher or lower wages but primarily one of insufficient social mastery of social production. To be sure, exploitation, which appears for the class in the form of low wages and poverty, are matters of primary importance for the revolutionary precisely in this form, since suffering is a powerful incentive for 'the class in itself' to become a 'class for itself'. However, they are neither issues that can be solved in the present society nor ones that would require the whole attention of the revolutionary. As for the future, the terms of his own theory precluded focusing on the social question. For one thing, together with the withering away of the state, Marx's theory also aimed at the withering away of *societas* in its traditional sense. Furthermore, the technical precondition of his prediction about 'the end of pre-history', namely the abolition of scarcity, the absolute satisfiability of (basically moderate and static) needs, as well as the philosophical precondition of the new social place allotted to the emancipated producer either outside production or, at the very worst, in a drastically curtailed 'realm of necessity', effectively voided 'the social question' of its traditional contents. Marx devised a theory of the future which had no message for the advocates of the social question: in this projected future there were no social issues.

The socialists who were genuinely involved with the social problem which had been so deliberately neglected by Marx were either members of the English branch (above all Owen) or the social democrats in the last quarter of the nineteenth century. The latter's position on the social question was straightforward and consistent, albeit lacking in theoretical sophistication and totally exempt from metaphysical concerns. Whatever a new 'workers' state' (which the social democrats still believed in) could bring in the future, they nevertheless felt it their duty to cope then and there with the poverty, low life expectancy and ignorance of their own constituencies. They were convinced that this task could, at least to a considerable degree, be accomplished within the framework of the existing society. Moreover, as offspring of the Enlightenment and completely impervious to dialectical niceties, the social democrats saw no inherent reason for regarding a better lot and a higher level of education as detrimental to the class consciousness of the proletariat. In fact, their experiences taught them to profess the exact opposite view. Nor was the second part of their self-appelation a camouflage. For social democrats, it was common knowledge that democracy alone could bring gradual and progressive changes in the social question. Therefore, they simply joined the host of petitioners who appealed to the state for improvements in the social issues.

It was the privilege of the latecomer, the communist revolutionary, to forge a fraudulent metaphysics of the social question and pursue it to its catastrophic conclusions. Discussing *in extenso* whether or not this new revolutionary adhered strictly to Marx or otherwise, would be a fairly sterile debate. It will suffice to say that on the one hand, as previously mentioned, Marx's philosophical critique of capitalism was not targeted to the social question, but was aiming rather at a radical anthropology and at transforming *societas* into an 'association of producers'. On the other hand, there can be little doubt that certain features of Marx's original theory, namely, his 'scientific' forecast of a 'guaranteed society'; his highly ambiguous theory of exploitation (which sometimes seemed to suggest that the expropriation of the exploiter will *in uno actu* abolish poverty, while at other times the theory explicitly denied this possibility), fuelled the attempts at forging a metaphysics of the social question.

The term 'fraudulent' is not meant to introduce a conspiracy theory into the interpretation of history. Our aim is only to expose the dangerous structure of a particular power politics which initially, but only initially, sincerely embraced certain commitments as well as raised relevant issues with regard to 'the social question'. Moreover, these politics manifested an incomparably livelier interest in social issues than did Marx himself, for the simple reason that, unlike Marx, communist power politicians had to mobilize masses. The relevant point brought out by the communist position on 'the social question' lies in their criticism of the formal character of liberties, even if the communist counter-proposal of a 'substantive freedom' is nothing but demagoguery. For no one can deny without bias that the underpaid and overworked masses of industrial workers who constituted the bulk of the communist constituency, never had the time, the energy, the means nor the education for participating in the practice of political liberties. For these workers, therefore, freedom remained an abstract, rather than an actualizable, possibility. It has added to the momentum of the communist position that the social democrats often overlooked, or embellished this structural weakness of democracies with a capitalist organization of the economy. Communism thrived on the insufficient political radicalism of social democracy.

However, the conclusions drawn from this correct and relevant premiss have gradually been translated into the vocabulary of a fraudulent metaphysics of the social question by the communist ideology. (Not to mention the additional fact that their systematic apology for the horrendous reality of the Soviet Union under Stalin and after renders the sincerity of the communist commitment to the social question thoroughly questionable.) Their first conclusion was the categorical rejection of democracy as a 'lie', as 'bourgeois', a mere deceptive facade drawn in front of substantive inequalities and exploitation. In this sense, they remained true heirs to Marx's own critique of democracy. Their second conclusion was the promise of a society which would allegedly solve the social question as a whole. This conclusion can already be termed fraudulent because the communists in power were invariably and exclusively preoccupied with a new, streamlined type of social control and with their project of forced and rapid industrialization. However, a society of control and, above all, politics of forced industrialization normally imposes terrible, and as a rule, superfluous additional sufferings on to the populace. The next two steps of the doctrine have transformed the false promise into a systematic, and transparently fraudulent metaphysics. In the wake of Marx, Marxism-Leninism operated with an interconnected and progressive series of 'social formations' into which they now inserted a new link between capitalism and the emancipated society projected by Marx: 'communism'. The new 'social formation', socialism, apparently had one historic task, that of becoming the society *par excellence* that would solve the social question once and for all. Devising a society with the explicit mission of becoming a 'counter-society', that is, one distinguished from every other hitherto existing society by its hidden potential for solving that which has permanently remained unsolved, was unquestionably an exercise in metaphysics. The last step, the crowning act, was the theoretical invention of the 'new man', *Homo Sovieticus*,[4] whose *differentia specifica* was that he/she could bear the crippling burdens of the social experiment not only with equanimity and passive obedience but with internal satisfaction and optimism as well. Optimism was supposed to originate from the new man's unassailable belief that his/her social problems had in fact been solved and his/her affairs only needed 'further perfecting'.

As the events of the last decades attest, however, the new metaphysics of the social question had very little pragmatic success in taming the actual men and women of Soviet societies. The public spaces of these societies are now full of the ever louder airing of grievances by the disenchanted and the socially dissatisfied, to which more recently even some of their leaders add their critical and self-critical remarks. And yet, this metaphysics has achieved a stunning ideological victory owing to its shrewd perception of the anthropological bases of 'dissatisfied society'. The misleading radicalism of the postulate and belief that there is an integrated 'social question' *in abstracto* to be solved by a particular set of measures fully and for all eternity, was initially a communist invention. But it has outlived the general belief in the viability of communist projects and blueprints. Its relative longevity is due to one factor: it serves well the bad faith of the permanent and massive frustration of 'dissatisfied society'.

III

All attempts at a radical democratic answer to the social problem, which opposes itself equally to the conservative liberal option for discarding the social issues and the communist metaphysics of the social question, have to depart from the recognition of a whole set of characteristic features of the syndrome in modernity. These are its irreducible pluralism; the permanent and irresistible growth of its scope and dimensions; the need for continually putting the pressing issues on the political agenda; the simultaneous conviction that the social question as a whole cannot possibly be solved in any given state of affairs; the recognition of a publicly and freely articulated concept of social justice as our guide in weighing and assessing particular social issues; and finally, the priority of freedom in the process.

A quick glance at every random list of present social issues will immediately attest to the irreducible plurality of the allegedly homogenous 'social question'. The traditional contrast between wealth and poverty has remained on top of every list. Here, 'poverty' is in part understood as 'culturally defined' or relative poverty, and in part as the absolute poverty of those living below the biological threshold of physical self-reproduction. The cause of this contrast is these days widely interpreted in terms of income differences and differences in property status, and deemed, at least by those who compile lists like these, socially unjust. The unequal access to institutions, which is to say, to the 'practice of freedom', comes next on this list, which in societies devoid of institutionalized racial and social discriminations, is normally considered to be primarily rooted in the sphere of education. Racial and ethnic-religious discrimination figure among the most dramatic social issues in the post-war world. Gender and age discrimination, that is, the unequal and unjust situation of women and children in the household, in legislation as well as in the actual management of political, cultural and business affairs, has also transpired as one of the major social grievances in the last decades. The dramatic inequalities between various regions of the world, threatening the global equilibrium with destructive wars, has also been put on the agenda of social issues in the aftermath of the collapse of the colonial system and the frighteningly destructive qualities of the new weapons. Population growth, traditionally one of the 'most natural' factors of human existence, has now attained to the rank of a social issue and has become a major matter of social legislation. So has the problem of health, yet another natural factor of human existence.

The most superficial, but unbiased, study of these issues leads one to the inevitable conclusion that, while these issues as a whole have to be addressed by politics, they are in the first place highly heterogeneous and the methods devised for the solution of one are therefore probably inadequate for tackling another. Furthermore, the belief that one can somehow solve them *in toto* and for all time can only be a false promise and not a realistic programme. We have been witnessing for decades the emergence of an important and influential social experiment for addressing 'the social question' as a whole: the welfare state. This state is distinguished by two positive features from what we have hitherto termed a 'fraudulent metaphysics': it is based on freedom, on the procedures of liberal democracy, and second, its dominating ideology is a sceptical brand of liberalism or social democracy which has no penchant for holding out the promises of a paradise on earth. And yet, the structural weaknesses of the welfare state, which are due to the exclusive emphasis on the social question, are well known and have been widely discussed. In the main, they can be found in the dominant paternalistic authority of the state over society which, albeit benevolent, paralyses citizen activity and cultural dynamism.

The existence of the welfare state raises the problem of whether, and to what degree, politics *sui generis* still exist in a society where 'the social question' has become the major focus of political activity.[5] And yet, the relative autonomy of the political sphere can still be perceived and ascertained in the following areas. Since a politically unified humankind is neither a feasible, nor a particularly desirable perspective, the defence of the nation state, as well as defining its role in the world, will remain a purely political task. Formulating the priorities in the process of solving particular social issues, as well as ensuring the compatibility of their solution with the overriding principle of freedom, is equally an immanently political concern. Devising and promoting new cultural patterns cannot be reduced to a merely social and non-political activity either. Finally, the rational guidance of society over economic growth and economic dynamics, or, in other words, the elements of planning, have become, despite the spectacular fiasco of the Soviet system of centralized state planning, a vivid political concern of a growing number of citizens, quite apart from the social consequences of this economic growth.

The irreducible heterogeneity of distinct social issues elicits the typical alternative of our century, that is, 'reform of revolution', which becomes even more misleading with respect to the social question than in other fields. We witness a false dichotomy on this issue: those frightened by the violence and the invariably disheartening aftermath of revolutions, dogmatically insist that each and every social issue without exception can be solved by peaceful change. Those whose genuine, although hidden, telos is the new society of control with its allegedly superior rationality, equally dogmatically favour violent and abrupt change as the answer to unresolved social issues. We cannot see a general, all-embracing formula which would fit every dilemma and guide us at every juncture. On the one hand, certain social issues which have become highly politicized, can, if all avenues of compromise are blocked by a stubborn political opposition, only be solved by violence. In such cases, revolution is the only way to reform.[6] On the other hand, the present admissions of Chinese and Soviety leaders about the total inadequacy of the implemented measures in crucial areas of 'the social question' helps to shed light on the simple truth that certain violent revolutions which had been fought in the name of unsatisfied needs, wants and desires, hardly bring satisfaction with regard to a single issue. In short, the irreducible heterogeneity of social issues in modernity cannot be exhausted by a single magic formula or panacea.

The incessant growth of the number, volume and dimensions of social issues is an inevitable feature of modernity. One cannot even forecast, after the rise of environmentalism to the rank of a publicly recognized social issue, from which arena new social issues will emerge. For a considerable part of them stem from the very 'progress of modernity' itself, from the innovations, technological and social changes which we had earlier embraced without the faintest idea of the dilemmas they would generate.

The proliferation of social issues has a Janus-face, one of which is smiling and beneficial. For example, feminism has taught us the important lesson that certain issues cannot be adequately discussed in the private sphere; they have to become social in order to be emancipatory. The other face of this growth is, however, gloomy. For the constant widening of the list imposes an increasing, and often unbearable, burden upon the state. It also inevitably heightens the state's paternalistic supervisory omnipresence. And often the same people who push new social issues begin to resent both the increased (mostly fiscal) burdens and condemn the omnipresence of the state in their everyday life. The recurring flare-ups of neo-conservatism are only in part conditioned by class or group egoism. In part, they are the result of the hangovers that follow the triumphant recognition of new issues as 'social', and of the results which have been involved in rectifying them.

Our moderate scepticism towards the constant growth of social issues does not imply an altogether negative attitude. Growth has two unambiguously positive aspects. One of them is its 'signal function'. As long as the list widens, a particular society appears to function more or less normally. For after a lost 'total' war, a nationwide famine or natural catstrophe, the main issue is survival. And the mere survival of a society is not a social issue. Furthermore, growth can serve as one of the major guides in the ongoing social reviewing of economic growth, a review process which goes beyond market considerations.

IV

The first conclusion to be drawn from the above considerations is that reducing the inherent heterogeneity of social issues to the homogenous formula of 'the social question' is one of the most conspicuous examples of the inadmissable reduction of the complexity of modernity. The dangers of such an operation have been repeatedly pointed out both by Luhmann and Habermas. Abstract homogenization is misleading on each count. It suggests a single general recipe for treating widely divergent social malaises, many of which would simply not respond to the therapy, while others would show symptoms of malady precisely due to the therapy itself. It also serves as the theoretical justification of a fraudulent metaphysics.

The second conclusion is that making the solutions of all social issues conditional on a particular set of institutional changes is either illusory of deliberately misleading. Nationalization is the classic case in point. A certain degree or type of nationalization appears to remain a legitimate item of every leftist programme, with the proviso that it should not abolish market economy altogether nor, above all, should it lead to the totalitarian power of the state over society. In Great Britain, nationalization of a considerable sector of the economy after the war served the purpose of introducing far-reaching welfarist measures, a tremendously positive social reform. In other countries which have established classic versions of the welfare state, for example Sweden, formal nationalization of this scope and width was not necessary for this end. In yet another group of post-colonial states, almost total nationalization resulted in the spectacular increase in prosperity of the new greedy middle classes and in the almost criminal neglect of the social demands of the bulk of the populace. In Soviet societies, total state control of social life concluded in the ban on discussing 'the social question', which had been declared to have been resolved as a whole and for good. This issue was then put intermittently on the agenda once again for, as it has transpired, it has been altogether neglected rather than resolved. The recently emerging, more or less reliable, figures of the percentage of those living in these countries below the poverty line attest to the complete inefficiency of total nationalization as a remedy against social ills.

Finally, certain conclusions can be drawn about the much debated issue of the relationship between democracy and socialism, or 'democratic socialism'. These debates seem to be increasingly sterile to us for, among other reasons, the concept of 'socialism' is tacitly accepted in them as the equivalent of a brand-new society which has the mission of solving 'the social question' as a whole and for good. In so far as the latter is either impossible or a false promise, which is the bottom-line premiss of our train of thought, 'socialism' as a 'new formation' transcending modernity is a conceptual mythology. With this assertion, we do not wish to undermine the socialists' self-identity. Socialism as the self-appelation and self-characterization of particular actors as well as of different movements and political parties remains a relevant term in part because 'socialisms in the plural' are not linked only with social, but also with political and cultural issues. 'Socialisms' are of course inseparable from the embracing of particular social issues with the firm commitment of solving them as well as possible at a given level of civilization, national wealth, cultural expectation and the like. Moreover, the character of particular socialisms is ultimately determined by the particular social issues which they embrace. The latter can serve as at least one of the yardsticks for comparing particular socialisms with one another. In our view, 'socialisms in the plural' appear as so many divergent and heterogeneous attempts at *rearranging modernity*, but not as seeking its total transcendence and absolute negation. Socialisms of different kinds will then create a hierarchy of social issues on the basis of a free and ongoing discourse, instead of holding out the false promise to solve all of them exhaustively. Thus democracy or political freedom, both in its traditional and in several new and modified forms, would not appear as a principle external to some mysterous 'socialism' which can or alternatively cannot be combined with democracy, but which can also exist in itself. Political freedom transpires here as the absolute precondition of articulating social issues, as a *conditio sine qua non* of the various types of socialism. In un-freedom, only the chimera or the false promise of allegedly eternally solved social issues exists. Freedom is the real progenitor of socialisms. In this maxim an old Marxian dictum returns. In a society where movements freely forge the political options, where they are unhindered in elaborating the *political* principles or the hierarchy of *social* issues, where they entrust parties and the state with implementing their social expectations, the maxim of 'human self-management', which is relatively separated from the management, or administration, of things, might come true.

Notes

1 For the historical clarification of this thesis see F. Fehér, *The Frozen Revolution (an essay on Jacobinism)*, Cambridge University Press, Cambridge, 1987.

2 This position has hardly anything in common with Hannah Arendt's well-known thesis in *The Human Condition*. In her view, 'the social question', or 'the social domain' only emerged in an age when concerns of an economic nature started to transcend the frame of the household. These concerns, she believed, were bound to return to the domestic sphere or else a *constitutio libertatis* could not be established. Despite several of her insightful remarks, we are not identifying with her position, because to us the deletion of the 'social question' from the permanent agenda of modernity is both an impossible and a retrograde enterprise. Nor do we believe that Marx, as Arendt characterized him, ever became a philosopher of 'the social question' instead of a philosopher of freedom.

3 When we mention 'Marx's lifelong concern with alienation', we deliberately adopt one particular interpretation of his *oeuvre*, the so-called 'humanist' or anti-Althusserian interpretation. However, 'Marxology' is a marginal issue in this train of thought.

4 In mentioning *Homo Sovieticus*, we refer to M. Heller and A. Nekrich, *L'Utopie au Pouvoir*, Calmann-Levy, Paris, 1985. We agree with these authors as far as their critical morphology is concerned, but not with their theoretical premises and conclusions.

5 It was Mary McCarthy, a close friend of Hannah Arendt, who, in a debate on Arendt's famous thesis of the necessity of dispelling the social from the domain of the political, naively asked her: 'And what are we going to discuss in the future, once there will be no social issues in our politics?' Not surprisingly, Arendt was at a loss as to how to answer the question.

6 'Reform through revolution' appears to be the only future in South Africa. Due to the foolhardy opposition of the white minority to compromises of any kind, racial discrimination, a social issue, can apparently be abolished only through political revolution. Nor is this a leftist or radical option. Malcolm Fraser, the conservative ex-Prime Minister of Australia, adopts exactly this position on the basis of the well-known liberal postulate of 'right to evolution'.

9

Social Justice and its Principles

I

Let us, first, present a general and abstract formula of justice. It is general and abstract for all kinds of justice can be described by it. The formula reads as follows. 'The norms and rules which constitute a human cluster, should be applied consistently and continuously to each and every member of that cluster.' We are going to term this formula *the formal concept of justice*. The formula can be applied and fitted to all concrete instances of justice. One is just if one acts in accordance with the prescription contained in the formula. Conversely, one can be said to be acting unjustly whenever one either (a) applies norms and rules inconsistently, (b) applies them in a discontinuous manner, or (c) applies a norm or a rule other than the one which constitutes that particular human cluster to members of that cluster. To give an example, if you are a teacher and you correct the examination papers of your students, you assess them in accordance with certain rules of excellence which are valid for each and every student. If you give higher marks to some students because you like them more than others, you are inconsistent and thus acting unjustly. If you correct the papers by using a high standard in the morning and a lower standard in the afternoon, because your attention and concentration spans have diminished, then you infringe the principle of continuity, and are thus equally open to the charge of acting unjustly. Again, if your mark the papers consistently and continuously, but you use standards of political preference (instead of those of excellence), you fail to apply the very standard the particular institutional norms demand and thus also would be acting unjustly.

There are many different kinds of just or unjust acts. There are acts of judgement, acts of distribution, acts which grant or which withhold something, acts of reward or punishment, and many other kinds. Yet, justice or injustice can only be ascribed to an action which is performed in accordance with rules and norms. It follows from this that nature cannot be either just or unjust, although we sometimes, metaphorically, extend the use of such terms to nature. It also follows from this that *feelings* in themselves cannot be termed either just or unjust. Finally, it follows from this, that actions can be just or unjust only if they can be *compared* and, incidentally, *ranked*. This is why *equality* and *inequality* are the constitutive values of justice. That which is *unique* can neither be compared nor ranked, and, obviously, unique entities cannot be each other's equals or unequals either. Human personalities are doubtless unique and therefore, no human person is, as a whole, equal to any other human person; persons in their totalities are simply different and as such incommensurable. Yet if we compare human beings who belong to the same cluster, we are no longer comparing them as wholes but merely from the perspective of a norm or rule, that is, in one respect only. Thus, if we assert, in the spirit of the Declaration of Human Rights, that all human beings are born equal, we certainly do not mean that they are all alike. What we mean is rather that all humans are born as members of the universal cluster called humankind and that they deserve equal recognition of their humanness by virtue of their belonging to the same (universal) cluster. Equality is not a substance; both equality and inequality are constituted by norms and rules and by them alone. It should be noted in advance that norms and rules are not merely constitutive of human clusters – some norms are trans-clusteral. In the present context, however, we shall confine our discussion to the former only.

To be just is a moral virtue, to be unjust is a serious moral shortcoming irrespective of whether the norms and rules a person applies consistently and continuously, or fails to apply properly, have anything to do with moral matters. Every teacher knows that the students who write the best examination papers are not necessarily those who deserve the best marks, yet one acts justly only if one marks in accordance with the rules and norms appropriate to the particular context; in this case, the norms and rules appropriate to examinations. Justice is a cold virtue, for it requires impartiality.

The norms and rules which constitute human clusters are different in kind. Nonetheless we can typify them according to the *ideas* of justice they embody. Ideas of justice are general principles of comparison and ranking. Different societies are characterized by different, all-encompassing or decisive ideas of justice. Certain other ideas of justice may inhere in the very *substance* of a particular institutional complex. The following maxims comprise the principal ideas of justice: to each the same thing; to each according to his/her merits; to each according to his/her excellence; to each according to his/her rank; to each what is due to him or her by virtue of his/her belonging to a particular essential category. The idea 'to each according to his/her rank' is clearly an all-encompassing idea of justice in premodern, high civilizations, though it has little or no relevance to our own modern world. All other ideas of justice, however, are of great relevance to present-day societies, where they serve as guiding principles for the norms and rules of a great number of institutions. The relevance of the ideas of justice will be highlighted when we turn to the question of 'social justice' below. At this stage we should like to take the discussion of the ideas of justice a little further.

Not all ideas of justice can be applied to each and every sphere or institution within a particular society. Some spheres exclude certain ideas of justice either by definition or *normatively* (that is, because we have already chosen certain norms and rules which exclude them). Returning to our earlier example, we can see that in marking examination papers the *only idea* that can regulate the norms and rules is the idea 'to each according to his/her excellence'. Were we to apply to marking the idea 'to each the same', we would no longer mark at all. In other words, the idea 'to each the same' is excluded from this institution *by definition*. When we turn to political rights, however, the idea 'to each the same' is of vital importance. Without doubt, other ideas too could be the case, for instance the idea 'to each according to his/her excellence'. But we do not want them to be the case – this is why we exclude all other ideas except the one: 'to each the same' *normatively* from regulating norms concerning political rights.

The question may arise as to why we have not included the principle 'to each according to his/her needs' among the ideas of justice. We have excluded it quite deliberately because, contrary to widespread belief, this principle is *not* an idea of justice. Rather, this principle enjoins us to go *beyond* justice. Since all persons are unique, they cannot be equalized, and thus the satisfaction of all needs of all persons cannot rest on comparison and ranking. The principle 'to each according to his/her needs' is therefore more appropriately rendered in the following terms: 'to each according to his/her *uniqueness*'. In excluding the principle 'to each according to his/her needs' from the ideas of justice, we do not mean to imply that the ideas of justice have no relevance to needs. The idea 'to each the same thing', for instance, would govern that cluster of needs which ought to be satisfied to an equal degree for all people. The idea 'to each what is due to him or her by virtue of his/her belonging to an essential category' applies to those needs which arise in particular contexts such as a sick person's right to socially guaranteed medical care or an unemployed person's right to unemployment benefits. These examples indicate that this particular idea of justice is employed on a broad social scale in welfare states. In fact, there is only one idea of justice – the idea 'to each according to his/her merits (or demerits)' – that disregards needs completely. An undeserving person may need to be praised to the same degree as a deserving one, but the application of this idea of justice serves to exclude the undeserving need from consideration.

Up to this point we have briefly discussed aspects of the formal concept of justice. We have argued that all kinds of justice can ultimately be brought under the formula which holds that 'the norms and rules which constitute a human cluster should be applied consistently and continuously to each and every member of that cluster.' We have also argued that the norms and rules of a cluster can themselves be informed and guided by various ideas of justice. We should now like to take the argument a step further, by drawing a distinction between the concept of *static* justice and that of *dynamic* justice.

Our conception of justice is *static* whenever norms and rules are seen as unproblematic; whenever they are taken for granted and neither queried nor tested. In this context, we confine the terms 'just' or 'unjust' to the *application* of norms and rules. We do not, for instance, question whether it is just or unjust to assess students in terms of the results of examination papers nor do we question whether or not it is just to remunerate certain types of work with higher wages and salaries than other types of work. Justice is done only if good examination papers obtain good marks and bad ones bad marks, and, similarly, highly qualified work is remunerated with higher salaries than work which requires no qualification. Injustice is said to result if such rules are overturned that is, whenever social power (such as wealth or political influence) or personal favour (motivated by greed or sympathy) leads to an inconsistent application of rules. If tax laws are deemed just, tax evasion or tax avoidance is, by definition, unjust.

When the taken-for-grantedness of norms and rules is lost, that is, when we begin to question them and test their validity, our conception of justice is a *dynamic* one. Let us suppose that there are certain legally established or socially accepted norms and rules which may or may not be consistently applied. We can disregard the issue of application and designate the norms and rules, as they stand, as unjust. New, alternative, norms and rules have to be substituted for them. Both aspects of this assertion are of equal importance here. The rejection of certain norms and rules does not in itself fulfil the requirement of dynamic justice; alternative norms and rules which, to our minds, are just, must also be proposed and tested. Thus, were the rules pertaining to 'the just conduct of war' seen to be unjust and were we to propose instead that the conduct of war should not be regulated *at all* by any norms and rules, we would not be operating with a dynamic conception of justice. Similarly, our concept would not be that of justice if we rejected all social regulations as unjust by definition, on the grounds that everyone ought to be free to do whatever they wish. The formula dynamic justice reads as follows: 'not *this* is just, but *that* would rather be just.'

To make evaluative statements like 'this is just', 'this is unjust' in the context of a static conception of justice, is implicitly to make a claim about an existing social consensus (though, of course, this may not be a factual social consensus; something which rarely comes about.) Yet if we contend that the existing norms and rules of a particular kind are unjust and that an alternative set of norms and rules would be just, we are drawn into a *social conflict*, for behind claims to justice and injustice there always lie socially relevant groups. Thus, when we seek for and claim a social consensus, we express our desire, or our conviction, that at least the majority of our fellow-citizens will accept our alternative set of norms and rules as more just. Furthermore, we express the desire that the alternative use of norms and rules be substituted for the existing ones. In other words, we wish to transform our concept of justice from a dynamic one into a static one.

Static justice can therefore best be characterized as an *empirical human universal*. This means that there can be no society without static justice. Dynamic justice, by contrast, is not an empirical universal. There are still several communities in which all norms and rules are permanently taken for granted and conflicts over the kind of justice which is embedded in the existing set of norms and rules, never emerge. Whilst in premodern societies social conflicts centred on competing claims to justice were very much exceptional rather than normal occurrences, in modern societies this constellation has changed dramatically. Dynamic justice has attained a permanent place in our lives. We could even say, somewhat paradoxically, that in modern societies, at least in the west, dynamic justice has become a static element in that its presence is taken for granted. We are permanently questioning and testing the justice of one set of norms and rules against another. In such societies, there are very few norms and rules which are regarded as completely just by everyone.

How do we know that certain norms and rules are unjust and that other norms would be just or more just? This question could, of course, be rejected as irrelevant, and reformulated, as it was by Thrasymachus in Plato's *Republic*, in a relativistic manner: each and every social group follows its own interest and calls 'justice' that which best fits this interest. The stronger the group, the more the interests of that particular group coincide with what is regarded as just. On this view, right is might. However, if claims to justice are treated in this nominalistic or relativistic manner, all discussion concerning the nature of justice would indeed be irrelevant. Yet the argument is flawed. Even if we were to accept the proposition that all groups which contest the justice of an existing norm or rule are motivated by their needs and interests, it would not follow from this that an alternative set of norms and rules would only be *termed* more just by virtue of the underlying needs or interests. In fact, they could as easily be more just as more unjust. Needs and interests do motivate conflicts centred on claims to justice but they *can not determine* whether particular norms and rules are in fact just or not. What determines justice then? Those who reject relativistic or nominalistic arguments normally point to certain *absolutes* or ultimate yardsticks – such as divine laws or laws of nature – it is to them that social norms and rules must be compared.

In the modern world, belief in divine justice has been widely shattered and no longer provides most of us with any guidance, and theories of 'natural law' have been repeatedly discredited. This, however, does not mean that we are lacking in ultimate yardsticks. The emergence of the modern world has, in fact, been accompanied by the universalization of two values. These are the values of *freedom* and *life*. The value of freedom has become universalized to a degree that it has become a *value-idea*. By 'value-idea' we mean a value whose opposite cannot be chosen as value. The value of life, although not universal to the same degree, has also become a value-idea in western modernity. The universality of a value-idea means that it ought to be extended to all human persons. Norms and rules of justice can satisfy the requirement of value-ideas if they are informed by these ideas. The ultimate, absolute yardstick by which the justice or injustice of norms and rules can be measured, could then be formulated as follows: 'equal freedom for all; equal life-chances for all'. Not equality, but life and freedom are the unconditional values of modernity. Equality is a conditional value in the sense that it needs to be related to the values of freedom and life in order to give it meaning. Equality in misery or in un-freedom, for instance, is of negative value.

If we look back at the history of dynamic justice from a modern point of view, we can detect a common feature in each particular conflict which has arisen over claims to justice. Those who insisted that certain norms and rules were unjust and who argued for the institutionalization of new, alternative ones, have always raised the claim that a particular group of people should enjoy the same freedoms, or the same life-chances, as another group. In claiming the same amount of freedom, they made a claim to *political* justice in claiming the same amount of life-chances, their claims were ones for *social* justice. As a rule, such conflicts were settled either by force, by negotiations or by discourse. The universalization of the values of freedom and life has modified the tradition in two, equally important, respects. Firstly, equal freedom is no longer claimed for one particular group but for all social groups. Likewise, equal life-chances are no longer claimed for one particular group but for all. Secondly, in so far as freedom is understood as universal, force cannot be accepted as the pre-eminent or even decisive means by which to settle social and political conflicts. This is self-evident; if it is force that settles conflicts, one group of people will not accept the alternative norms and rules freely but only under the constraint of force. The institutionization of norms and rules must therefore be the outcome of negotiation or discourse. Force can be used only to the extent necessary to ensure that a group of people listens to the arguments of others. Negotiation is a procedure in which conflicts of interest are settled by compromise. Discourse is a procedure in which value conflicts are settled consensually by rational argument. Norms and rules in modern times can be regarded as just only in so far as they are accepted as just by everyone concerned as a result of a value discourse in which everyone has recourse to the universal values of freedom and life. This is the idea of the just procedure. It would be a sign of extreme optimism to believe that in our present-day world all norms and rules will be established by such a procedure. Yet a seeming remoteness is not grounds for not seeking to approximate to the just procedure whenever possible.

A few important consequences would seem to follow from this idea of dynamic justice. Firstly, philosophers or social scientists, as intelligent or well informed or as sincere or committed as they may be, are not authorized to outline any blueprint for a just society if by this they intend that it should serve as an incontestable, ultimate model as such. Of course, as citizens, they have the same right as any other citizen to argue for their own projects of social and political justice. They may offer blueprints if such gestures are made as contributions to discussion and other persons concerned with such projects are free to accept or reject them. In so far as he/she recommends his/her blueprint, the social scientist offers a *social service*, not an 'expert opinion', and interested parties should always have the opportunity to accept or reject it according to their needs, values, life experiences and interests. Secondly, there is no blueprint for a just society which would be valid (accepted as just) for every nation, every culture, every way of life. Human cultures are different, lifestyles are different: the same norm which may be just in one country, in the context of a particular way of life, could still be unjust in another country with different traditions and cultures.

II

Let us now turn to the special problem of social justice. We have suggested above that wherever and whenever norms and rules are rejected as unjust and alternative norms and rules are recommended as just – that is, whenever we are working with a dynamic conception of justice – a claim is being made for the extension or narrowing down of freedom and life-chances. Static justice differs from dynamic justice in that with the former norms are taken for granted and, by implication, also accepted as just. Yet if persons protest against the inconsistent application of those norms, they too make a claim for the equality of their life-chances and, incidentally, for the equality of their freedom. If parents turn a blind eye to the misbehaviour of one of their children but reprimand the others for the same act, this would constitute a matter of discrimination against the freedom and life-chances of the other children. If men and women are treated as equals by law, yet women get lower wages for their work and less recognition in their person, the freedoms and life-chances of women are curtailed in comparison to the freedoms and life-chances of men. It follows from this that the institutionalization of new (more just) norms is not, in itself, sufficient; their consistent and continuous application is also a precondition of social justice. This is all the more important for people's attitudes to social and political regulations can be similar to their attitude to pure moral regulations. That is, they can accept such regulations as just, right or good and still fail to apply them accordingly.

We have already argued above that if norms and rules are under attack from the standpoint of freedom, the contestations over types of justice are pre-eminently political and if norms and rules are under attack from the standpoint of life-chances, such contestations are pre-eminently social. 'Social justice' is thus related to life-chances. A group claiming 'social justice' claims life-chances equal to those of another group, or at least an increase in the life-chances of its members in comparison with the life-chances the members of another group, or all other groups, enjoy. Obviously, there is a strong connecting link between political and social justice. If a group achieves equal freedoms with another group, the possibility of improving the life-chances of its members also increases. Or, to formulate this the other way round: once political freedom is achieved, contestations over social justice can go on unabated. Claims to social justice have an important political implication as well: the more their life-chances increase, the more people can make use of political freedom and equality. Yet this is true only if political rights and freedoms exist. Life-chances can be equalized without having any impact at all on political freedoms: they can be equally zero or equally dictated by a small clique of dictators as was the case in the Kampuchea of the Khmer Rouge. This is why Rawls is right in emphasizing that political justice, as equality in freedoms, has a priority over all othe types of justice. Equal political freedoms and rights are just not because society is just or the political institutions of society are just, but because equality in political rights and freedoms includes the rights to both social and political contestations, and these rights are granted to all. In order to avoid any misunderstanding, let us emphasize again that equal freedoms and political rights for all members of a body politic do not put an end to conflicts about the justice of one or another particular political institution. However, such rights provide the framework within which both political and social conflicts can proceed via negotiation and discourse.

Western modernity is characterized by the relative independence of civil society from the state. The recognition of this structured feature gave rise to the belief that civil society is the locus of social action whereas the state is the locus of political action. Social conflict centres on state power. The Marxian theory that the state is but a superstructure of the economic base of a capitalist civil society reconfirmed the liberal view, although it certainly reversed the practical conclusions which follow from it. However, it has become clear, particularly in the twentieth century, after World War Two, that attributing social action to groups within civil society and political action to the state is an inadequate account of the nature of social and political action. There are at least two reasons for this. Firstly, the traditional issue of social justice, namely economic redistribution and welfare, has been incorporated into state policies. These days the electorate is more involved in the economic, fiscal and social policies of a party or a government than in their political programme proper. Secondly, social movement are increasingly orientated towards political issues or, more correctly, they tend to *politicize* social issues, by translating private grievances into public problems. Although redistribution is still a decisive question on the agenda of social justice, other issues have assumed equal prominence. Feminist movements, ecological movements, movements seeking to change the form of life, peace movements and the like introduce unorthodox and new problems into the public arena, and social and political questions begin to merge. Put simply, the issues which concern *life-chances*, the very issues which traditionally have been subsumed under the rubric 'social justice', have now become richer, more manifold and heterogeneous on the one hand, and increasingly politicized as 'public concerns' on the other.

We have already noted that traditionally claims to 'social justice' focused on the distribution and redistribution of wealth, the so-called problem of 'distributive justice'. Social rules which permitted the few to accumulate a vast wealth and which kept others permanently on the verge of starvation were frequently looked upon as unjust even in premodern societies. The poor revolted to get their daily bread, religions threatened the rich with divine retribution unless they gave away some of their wealth. Yet the distributive gap between the wealthy and the poor has remained with us, even if not always to the same extent. Egalitarian movements have also re-emerged in the modern world: Babeuf's and Buonarotti's egalitarian communism are modern and updated versions of the ancient tradition of 'natural justice'. As is well known, Marx rejected egalitarian communism as a form of generalized envy and, in addition, he contended that any claim for greater distributive justice is false and misleading. Distribution, so he argued, is at any rate secondary to production. Yet, these and similar speculations have never prevented workers and intellectuals, socialists, social democrats and American liberals from upholding the ideal of a more just distribution of material wealth, and nor have they prevented them from implementing certain new policies, from progressive taxation to welfare services, in order to blunt the edges of a blatant distributive injustice.

At the same time, 'distributive justice' itself has become far more broadly conceived than it had ever been. Following Luhmann's distinction, traditional societies can be termed 'stratified' and modern societies 'functionalist'. In a traditional society, it was the place occupied in the division of labour that determined the function a person performed; one was simply born into that station. In modern society, the order of determination occurs the other way round: the function one performs in the division of labour determines one's position in the patterns of stratification. It follows from this that the claim to social justice increasingly includes the claim for an 'equal start', that is, for an equality in life-chances. If the position occupied in a stratified social order depends on the function performed, the claim to social justice requires that everyone should have an equal opportunity to perform the kind of function he/she is best able to perform according to his/her talents, and not due to his/her position at birth. Since more rewarding and better-paid functions require higher education, the channels of education must be opened for all, and for all equally – hence the institutionalization of meritocratic rules such as 'to each according to his/her excellence'. The claim to social justice based on the idea of meritocracy lifted traditional ethnic and gender barriers. The gates of universities have been opened for all ethnic groups as well as for women.

Yet even in democratic welfare states where the claims of a modern 'distributive justice' have been institutionalized to a greater or lesser degree, blatant social injustices are still evident. As a result, a set of questions have been raised about the idea of social justice itself. Let us enumerate a few of them. Can the principle 'to each according to his/her excellence' really work within contemporary societies? Is the meritocratic principle in itself just or, rather, should it be combined with the egalitarian principle 'to each the same'? Can an approximative social justice be implemented at all by redistributing goods, services and opportunities? Should the state be the main agent of redistributive justice if this course leads to a paternalism which is detrimental to social action proper and to social responsibility and initiative?

It is generally recognized that the meritocratic principle does not work the way it should or could. No 'initial equality of life-chances' exists because the 'accident of birth' (whether someone was born into a wealthy or a poor family, into one of low or high aspirations, into one or another ethnic group, as a man or as a woman) strongly influences, even if it no longer completely determines, the chances for excelling in the performance of a function one does best. Yet the problem raised in the second question points further ahead. Why should people receive remunerations according to their excellence? What is excellence anyway? Everyone can excel in something. Why should a film actor be better paid than a garbage-collector if both excel in their occupation? A good deal of contemporary American liberal theory concentrates on the discussion of this problem. Rawls, whose theory of justice is the best known of these, has taken issue with the dogmatic application of the meritocratic principle. He argues for the acceptance of the so-called 'difference principle' according to which an excellent performance deserves higher remuneration only if it directly ameliorates the situation of the worst-off social cluster. Irrespective of whether alternative suggestions for distributive justice are informed by the idea 'to each according to his/her excellence' or by the combination of that idea with the principle 'to each the same thing', the social blueprint inherent in them is strikingly similar. Elsewhere, we have termed this blueprint the 'triad-model'. There are human atoms which start a race from the same starting point. Some of them win the race and end up in good positions. Others will loose the race, or eventually end up in the worst positions. The state, the third party to the bargain, and outside the race, takes from the winners a certain amount of the spoils and distributes it to the losers. Yet why should this model be taken for granted? Can we possibly imagine other social blueprints? In fact, we can easily imagine a society in which not individual atoms but collective entities participate in the race. We can equally easily imagine that different collective entities subscribe to different principles of distribution with the members of one community deeming one particular principle just, while the members of another community deem another principle just. It is by no means written in the stars that the state should take care of the elderly and the sick or even that it should organize all kinds of education. Nozick has made the point that the real Utopia is the blueprint of a world where all Utopias are realized. Obviously, life-chances and freedoms can be equal for anyone under such conditions. Nozik's proposal, however, has one shortcoming, and it is a decisive one: he rejects the practice of redistribution. Yet even if we have in mind different forms of life where each operates with specific modes of distribution which are considered just by its members, natural resources should still, to a greater or lesser extent, be re-distributed *among* such communities, social entities, forms of life. For without redistribution, one or another form of life would certainly be exposed to the danger of extinction and the norm of 'equal life-chances to all' would remain unfulfilled.

Every time we make a claim for alternative norms and rules of justice, we make a claim either for the perfection of an existing form of life or for a change of this form of life in one or another direction. Both attitudes are fruitful. In making a case for adopting the second course, we have not sought to imply that the first should be rejected. There are three principal reasons for our choosing the second course. Firstly, the more alternatives there are in ways of life, the better chance people have of living a good life. Secondly, the contemporary welfare state model, at least in Europe, is bedevilled by a severe crisis which invites experiences in social change if such experiences are freely chosen by those who participate in them. Thirdly, a future-orientated society cannot have any stability without being dynamic and thus changing; it can uphold its dynamism only if new imaginaries and Utopias exist and are represented by social actors.

Different alternative norms and rules can and should be argued for, yet none of these should be such as would decrease the amount of freedoms and life-chances which have already been achieved and secured by existing norms and rules. For if they do, their eventual implementation would be unjust. Before we recommend alternative regulations, we should first test them by using the universal normative ideas of 'equal freedom for all' and 'equal life-chances for all' as the standards of judgement. Yet even after we have tested such alternatives by universal standards, we cannot be certain that they are, or indeed will be, just. For there are many types of regulations, completely different in kind, which can equally live up to the exigencies of universal standards, which can equally bring us closer to the fulfilment of those standards. There is only one foolproof test for the justice, or the greater justice, of the recommended norms and rules, namely that they are freely accepted by everyone concerned, as a result of rational argument; that is, as a result of both negotiation and discourse. The more we approximate to such a procedure for argumentation, the more just our norms and rules will be. However, a completely just society is undesirable because 'complete social and political justice' would only be possible where no one could any longer claim that 'this norm or rule is unjust'. Under such conditions, dynamic justice would disappear, as would social dynamism in general. A completely static society is a negative, rather than a positive Utopia.

Up to this point, we have limited our discussion of social justice to modern democratic welfare states. Space does not permit us to go much further. However, one problem cannot be completely avoided even within this restricted framework. Members of democratic welfare states are also members of the human race. As human beings, they cannot cut themselves off from the rest of the world, and they should not attempt to do so. We live in an age of world history. Yet can we participate in performing just acts the world over? Furthermore, are we entitled to recommend alternative norms and rules we deem just to people with cultural backgrounds, traditions and histories so different from ours? There were times when both socialists and liberals believed that they were entitled to do so. Yet if we accept the formula that only those norms and rules are just which are accepted freely by everyone concerned, we must restrict our recommendations and suggest only two basic rules. The ones we have in mind concern political justice and social justice proper. We can raise claims concerning rules of international co-operation, for rules, once accepted, would permit the resolution of international conflicts by negotiation and discourse rather than by force (war). We can also recommend that all people, irrespective of their history, cultural traditions and the like, should enjoy political freedom, and the members of all countries should have equal political rights. For if this were the case, then the citizens of all states, participant members of all cultures, would be making their own claims to social justice, and they could institutionalize, at least in principle, the very rules and norms, *they*, and not we, consider to be just. We could lend active support to all movements which stand for political freedoms and equal rights. The above restrictions do not prevent us from giving our support to the victims of the most blatant social (distributive) injustices. 'Giving a hand' is still a gesture of charity in the spirit of the traditional (premodern) perception of distributive justice. Denizens of the western world cannot prescribe and nor can they even recommend, rules for the just distribution of wealth for the people of Ethiopia. Only the Ethiopian people are authorized to formulate and prescribe such norms and rules. Yet we are still authorized to claim that freedoms and rights should be granted to the people of Ethiopia for only under such conditions can they begin to contest existing claims to social justice (such as they are) with their own. And the denizens of the western world can still regard it as their social and moral duty to rescue the people of Ethiopia from starvation in the spirit of commiseration and charity.

10

Existentialism, Alienation, Postmodernism: Cultural Movements as Vehicles of Change in the Patterns of Everyday Life

The term 'culture', or 'civilization' was invented in the west as one universal among many. Yet, in comparison to other universals such as 'science', or 'freedom', the universal termed 'culture' has always had a pluralistic connotation. One discussed science or freedom, for example, and not 'western science', and 'western freedom', because the general understanding was that these good things were one and indivisible. On the other hand, one discussed 'western culture' because it has always been assumed that there were many other cultures alongside the western one, whether inferior or superior to it, or simply different from it. Irrespective of whether those cultures were regarded as superior or inferior, the relationships among cultures were always temporalized as well as historicized. Cultures follow one another, for example, and there is no way back to a previous one except via a nostalgic trip which is only open to the single individual. In this understanding, cultures were regarded as closed universes which either remained closed or, if they eventually did open up, were then thought to lose their distinctive features and would thus be vulnerable to subversion by the latest, i.e. western, culture. This view of 'alien' cultures coincided structurally with the cultural divisions within particular countries in the period of early capitalism. Aristocratic, genteel, grand- and petty-bourgeois and peasant forms of life were strictly distinct from one another. The debate on cultural inferiority versus superiority occurred unremittingly with the contenders consisting of the aristocracy, the gentry (in England) and the bourgeoisie.

Class culture in the nineteenth century was more than a mere figure of speech. Disraeli's famous dictum mentioned two nations which were not even in communication with one another. Early working-class movements, the trade unions and later the parties, whether or not they explicitly advocated the creation of a special working-class culture, all nevertheless strongly contributed to the emergence of such a culture. Class cultures as a rule were almost hermetically sealed with individuals only occasionally able to cross the borders between them. This crossing of cultural borders was extremely difficult, and not only for those at the bottom aspiring upwards. Henry James, for example, was a great chronicler of the immense difficulties encountered even by people of enormous wealth once they ventured to cross the cultural barriers which divided them from 'the ancient families'.

The modern division of labour, with its capacity to stratify society along functional lines, began to break down the strict segregation of class cultures as early as the end of the nineteenth century. Freelance intellectuals, artists in particular, were the first 'splinter groups'. These artists created 'Bohemia' with a specific cultural flavour, a form of life all their own, which was neither aristocratic, nor bourgeois nor for that matter working class, but simply different. The culture of 'Bohemia' gradually broke up the hermetic closure of various cultures on a global scale by virtue of the fact that 'Bohemians' of one country regularly borowed artistic material, elements, themes and motifs from the so-called aliens of other countries. Gauguin's islanders no longer resemble the 'noble savage'; they are like us with a difference.

Yet it was only after World War Two that the erosion of a network of class cultures became visible and cultural relativism unmistakably gained momentum. Forms of life and cultural patterns could now be freely chosen, particularly by the younger generation, and cultural habits which had previously been exclusively class-related were now becoming generally available. In addition, in this epoch, one also sees 'other cultures' begin to borrow lavishly patterns of behaviour, habits, etc. from western fashions. Of course, such a conspicuous parallel development begs for a multi-causal explanation. We have already mentioned the emergence of the functional division of labour as one factor in this development. Factors such as the birth of mass production, the rise of the mass media, decolonization, and the decrease in working hours in the centres of western and northern Europe, could also be mentioned.

Rather than focus on causes, however, we would like to discuss briefly what might be termed imaginary *institutions of signification* (to borrow the phrase of Cornelius Castoriadis). In our view, there have been three distinct waves in which new imaginary significations of ways of life have been created since World War Two. We will deliberately disregard those theoretical tendencies (e.g., structuralism) which have deeply influenced our vision of the world. Instead, we will focus on those world-views and philosophies which were carried by cultural movements. For it was in the movements themselves that life-patterns were changed and that a new group of cultures in everyday life began to be slowly created. Needless to say, we are not at the end of this trend, but sufficiently in the midst of it to be able to watch the main tendencies of its unfolding.

As a rule, each new generation of young men and women has taken the initiative from the previous generation, since the time of the French Revolution. However, the distinct patterns of action, aspiration and imagination amongst post-World-War-Two youth have been sharply dissimilar to those of former generations. More precisely, the patterns have been becoming increasingly different from generation to generation. Although intellectuals, philosophers, sociologists, writers and artists have had their share in launching these movements and in articulating their aspirations, the youth whom they address and the aspirations and self-perceptions to which they give voice are widely dissimilar to those of the earlier bourgeois splinter group, 'Bohemia'. Post-World-War-Two movements did not warm up the old clichés about the aesthetic life; their extravaganza was not aesthetic, but existential. To an even lesser extent did they regard themselves as the cohort of a new political elite. Whether or not they were politically orientated, these movements were not involved in attempts to change elites.

In a society increasingly characterized by a functional division of labour, the term 'young' becomes equivalent to 'pre-functional'. In other words, everyone who is not yet absorbed by a function within the division of labour, is young. Movements of the young start to attract and embrace youth from extremely different social milieus, irrespective of whether their later function is to be that of academic or social worker, self-employed or industrial worker, etc. The tendency for the social 'absorbing power' of movements to widen is clearly in evidence. The cultural trend of 'punk' is a strong case in point.

However, pre-functional existence is at the same time pre-stratificational existence. As such, it allows for forms of life to develop which no longer have the characteristics of class cultures. Institutionalized function performance no longer suffices for preforming ways of life, as 'being a bourgeois' or 'being a worker' once did. This is why people cannot shed the vestiges of a particular 'youth culture' once they are settled in a social function. Certain elements of their own youth culture will continue to shape their lifestyles as adults. It is easy to ascertain that this is indeed the case. The transition from traditional class cultures to modern culture was destined to give birth to the most violent generational conflict modern men and women have ever known, and this dramatic process repeats itself wherever there are still traditional class cultures. However, once fathers and mothers themselves have been shaped by a modern movement, generation conflict between them and their children will be relatively mild, even if they disapprove of each other's values and ways of life. The softening of the generation conflict is but one sign among many of the structural changes in which new cultural movements are embedded.

Three consecutive generations have appeared since World War Two: the *existentialist* generation, the *alienation* generation and the *postmodernist* generation, to employ the terms of their own self-description. Modern cultural movements appeared in waves, and this happened for the simple reason that each new generation had to 'come of age' in the sense of creating a new 'imaginary institution' before it could take over the torch from the former generation. The first wave began its career immediately after the war and reached its zenith in the early fifties. The second wave was launched by the events of the mid-sixties and reached its peak in 1968, but continued to expand until the mid-seventies. The third movement arose in the eighties and has not yet reached its zenith. The second movement grew out of the first, and the third from the second, both in the sense of continuation but also in the sense of reversing the signs of the previous movement. In responding to one another, *each wave continues the pluralization of the cultural universe in modernity as well as the destruction of class cultures*. Furthermore, *each wave gives a new stimulus to the structural change in intergenerational relationships*. The latter is not quite independent from the former, for structural change in inter-generational relationships is yet another pattern of everyday life which points towards cultural relativism.

'Wave' and 'generation' are more precise terms than 'movement'. Although waves consist of cultural and social movements, certain movements continue through generations in a direct line instead of appearing in waves; feminism is the prime example. At the peak of the waves, movements which are 'fellow travellers' of the main trend tend, as a rule, to merge with the former, only then to be disconnected from them in an intermediary standstill. In addition, a wave is broader than the sum total of movements which emerge with it and which merge into one another at their peak. As a rule, movements meet with resistance, they provoke counter-movements, but even the counter-movements themselves display the characteristics of the waves which have brought them to the surface. And perhaps more interestingly, even those people, those forms of social action and those institutions which apparently have nothing to do with the 'waves', still have something in common with them. For they too participate in those changes in the social 'imaginary institution' of which the wave is an expression. It may seem far-fetched to associate the Falklands War and its *modus operandi* with postmodernism. And yet the war – the behaviour of the marines, the press reports and the like – seemed to be a deliberate quotation from World War One. It was as if the participants were purposefully quoting Renoir's celebrated movie, *La Grande Illusion*, as they imitated the valiant and chivalrous officers fighting duels of honours in the age of modern technology.

The *existentialist* generation was the first and the narrowest. The rapidity with which Sartre's message, though not necessarily his philosophy, caught the minds of the young in western Europe, and to some extent in central and southern Europe, was in itself not completely unprecedented. The Romantic movement had spread just as swiftly, over a century before. What was unprecedented, however, was the character of the movement, namely the *circumstance*, realized only in retrospect, that the existentialist wave was the first in a series of the most striking phenomena of western history in the second half of the twentieth century. The unprecedented character of the movement was due to its historical setting. This movement, like Romanticism, initially appeared as a *revolt of subjectivity* against the ossification of bourgeois forms of life, against the normative and ceremonial constraints rooted in this way of life. The rebellion of subjectivity did have political implication but one no more explicit than in previous Romantic movements. But prior to its emergence there had been the cataclysmic experience of totalitarianism, which made the life experience of contingency, so typical of modernity, an experience of personal freedom as well. However, the freedom of the existing, contingent person no longer sufficed in its capacity as *the* notion of freedom. Freedom had to be politicized. To this we must add the guilt of colonization and the experience of decolonization. In this experience, the politicization of freedom and the relativization of (western and bourgeois) culture were combined. All this swept through Europe in a series of cultural practices. 'Shocking the bourgeois' is precisely the gesture that makes men and women in revolt dependent on the bourgeois. But in the extentialist wave this famous *épater* was no longer present. What mattered now was doing things in our own way, practising our own freedom. Young men and women, intoxicated by the atmosphere of unlimited possibilities, began to dance existentially, love existentially, talk existentially, etc. In other words, they were intent on breaking free.

The alienation generation, which reached its peak in 1968, was both a continuation and a reversal of the first wave. Their formative experience was not the war but the post-war economic boom and the consequent widening of social possibilities. Their exerience, further- more, was not the dawn but the dusk of subjectivity and freedom. While the existentialist generation, despite its discovery of alienation, the lifelessness of modern institutions and the senselessness of contingency, had nevertheless been a rather optimistic breed, the alienation generation began in despair. Precisely because this generation took seriously the ideology of plenty, it rebelled against the complacency of industrial progress and affluence, as well as claiming for itself the sense and the meaning of life. Freedom remained the main value, however, and unlike the existentialist generation the alienation generation has remained committed to collectivism. The quest for freedom was a common pursuit.

Though an outgrowth of despair, the alienation generation became affirmative by virtue of the process in which different movements merged in the peak of this wave. In this merger literally nothing was left as it had been before. One movement made a plea for the extension of the human experience into taboo areas (and promoted the 'radical' cult of drugs, causing untold damage); the other made a claim for expanded families; yet another advocated the return to the simplicity of rural life; while still others supported sexual, or gay, liberation. Some movements raised concrete political objectives, while others were involved in experimental theatre, happenings, permissive education or in the advocacy of the slogan 'small is beautiful'. It is practically impossible to list all the issues and practices through which the second wave of the cultural movement made inroads into the perception and self-perception of modern western civilization.

As a social theory, postmodernism was born in 1968. In a manner of speaking, postmodernism was the creation of the alienation generation disillusioned with its own perception of the world. It can be argued that the defeat of 1968 was the reason for this disillusionment (if there was such a defeat, which remains an open question). However, one can also maintain that postmodernism had already appeared in the very beginnings of the 1968 movements, particularly in France, and that it therefore should simply be regarded as the continuation of the former. But whatever happened on the theoretical scene, the movements themselves seemed to disappear. The very same theorists who continued to relay the message of the alienation generation made speeches about the final defeat of social movements. Meanwhile, something else occurred. While the external signs of the movements vanished, there was still a movement; or rather, there were several, but they were invisible because they were essentially psychological and interpersonal. These movements increasingly saturated human relationships with their message to such an extent that they altered the social fabric from which they had emerged.

Postmodernism as a cultural movement (not as an ideology, theory, or programme) has a simple enough message: anything goes. This is not a slogan of rebellion, nor is postmodernism in fact rebellious. As far as everyday life is concerned, there are many and various things and patterns of life against which modern men and women can or should rebel, and postmodernism indeed allows for all sorts of rebellion. However, there is no single great target for collective and integrated rebellion. 'Anything goes' can be read as follows: *you* may rebel against anything you want to rebel against but let *me* rebel against the particular thing I want to rebel against. Or, alternatively speaking, let me not rebel against anything at all because I feel myself to be completely at ease.

For many, this boundless pluralism is the sign of conservatism: are there not crucial, focal issues which demand rebellion? And yet the truth is that postmodernism is neither conservative nor revolutionary nor progressive. It is neither a wave of rising hope nor a tide of deep despair. It is a cultural movement which makes distinctions of this kind irrelevant. For whether conservative, rebellious, revolutionary or progressive, all can be part of such a movement. This is so not because postmodernism is apolitical or anti-political, but rather because it does not stand for particular politics of any kind. Cultural relativism, which began its rebellion against the fossilization of class cultures as well as against the 'ethnocentric' lionization of the 'only-right-and-true', which is to say the western heritage, has succeeded. Indeed, it has succeeded so completely that it is now in a position to be able to entrench itself. Those who are now in the process of entrenching themselves are the members of the youngest generation who have learned their lessons and have drawn their own conclusions. Postmodernism is a wave within which all kinds of movements, artistic, political and cultural, are possible. We have already had several brand-new movements.

There have been movements with a focus on health, anti-smoking, body-building, alternative medicine, marathon-running and jogging. A movement of sexual counter-revolution has been developing. We have had and still have peace or anti-nuclear movements. Ecological movements are in full bloom. We witness the expansion of feminist movements, the movement for education reform and much else. The fashion magazines are perhaps the best indicators of the pluralist character of postmodernism. 'Fashion' as such no longer exists, or more precisely everything is, or many things are, fashionable at the same time. We no longer have 'good taste' or 'bad taste'. (Of course, one still might refer to having taste or not in the sense of being able to distinguish between the better and worse within the same genre.)

If postmodernism, then, is going to be absorbed by our culture as a whole, we will finally reach the end of the transformation which began with the existentialist generation after World War Two. This is not a prophecy about the end of movements, rather the opposite. What this statement does forecast is a situation in which concrete cultural transformations will take place in so far as such transformations are carried by one or another movement; however, the movements themselves will not occur in generational waves. These movements, finally, will not be the 'movements of the young'; they will not only be cross-class, but also cross-generational movements.

By way of introduction to the short story of the three generations which have created our present cultural 'imaginary institutions of signification', we have pointed out two decisive developments. We have stated that each wave continues the pluralization of the cultural universe in modernity as well as the destruction of class-related cultures. We have added that each wave has given a new stimulus to the structural change in intergenerational relations. We will now return to these fundamental questions in some detail.

What the three waves of cultural movements have achieved thus far and what can be expected to happen in the near future, will be discussed in the same breath. The transformation is uneven, for the present of one country is the future of another. No one factor can account for all of the differences in speed and character of the transformation. In matters of cultural transformations traditions of different provenance may accelerate or slow down a process. For example, traditional bourgeois forms of life are more entrenched in Germany than in Scandinavia. Yet even where the transformations are most spectacular, they are far from being close to completion. Class cultures are still very much in evidence. The European feeling of superiority has not evaporated and serious forms of generational conflict still exist. The bottom line is therefore a tendency rather than a *fait accompli*. A tendency is a possibility, and a latter can be regarded as less than 'reality'. But one could also agree with Aristotle that possibility stands higher than reality, that poetry is more true than history. The possibility mentioned here entails a small dosage of poetry, but it is based on the extrapolation of contemporary socio-economic features which have been discovered, discussed and corroborated through empirical data by sociologists such as Touraine, Offe and Dahrendorf.

The demise of class-related cultures can be explained in terms of the increase in consumerism. Previously, both bourgeois and working-class ways of life were centred on work performance. However, in what is termed these days 'post-industrial society', the centre of crucial life activities has become leisure time. As Dahrendorf has recently pointed out, not more than twenty-five per cent of the populace of the countries in the European Common Market perform socially necessary labour, which means holding a job or owning a business. Furthermore, function performance no longer provides the sufficient 'matter' from which a way of life can be constituted. In relation to life activity as a whole, function performance can be seen as fairly contingent, and is thus hardly the centrepoint of cultural identification. Rather, it is the *level* of consumption (the amount of money spent on consumption) that becomes the source of cultural identification. Cultural identification is therefore a quantitative rather than a qualitative issue. It was the deep conviction of the alienation generation that the *type* of preferred consumption had been socially generalized under the impact of the manipulation of tastes and desires by the mass media. In terms of this conception, everyone was manipulated into enjoying, being pleased with, and having a need for 'the same', irrespective of whether 'the same' referred to objects, products, forms of art, practices or whatever.

Although the growth of consumerism came to an abrupt halt with the advent of economic crises and depressions, and although the 'affluent society' proved to be far less affluent than the 'alienation generation' had previously assumed, the patterns which gave birth to the 'manipulation paradigm' have themselves not disappeared. But the outcome of general manipulation no longer assumes as gloomy a forecast as in earlier predictions. As so often happens, the prediction itself has changed the course of what was predicted. It seems an exaggeration, but in fact is not, that the wave of the alienation generation was, in this respect as well, the forerunner of the postmodernist generation. The spectre of 'mass society' in which everyone likes the same, reads the same, practises the same, was a short intermezzo in Europe and north America. What has indeed emerged is not the standardization and unification of consumption, but rather the enormous pluralization of tastes, practices, enjoyments and needs. The quantity of money available for spending continues to divide men and women, but so do the kinds and types of enjoyment, pleasure, practices which they seek. Instead of becoming the Great Manipulator, the media have become rather a catalogue for highly individualized tastes. More importantly, the different patterns of consumption have become embedded in a variety of lifestyles, 'each according to his or her preference', and of course, the means available to satisfy that preference.

At this point, we have to return to the general problem of cultural relativism. Non-western cultural patterns were first discovered by 'Bohemia'; the taste of the Bohemians was literally exotic. Today, 'alien' cultures are present at each and every level of everyday life. They have become embedded in our cultural practices; they have been assimilated, and they have become 'commonplace', as it were – from Chinese restaurants to Indian dresses, from African hairdos to Latin American novels. However bizarre it may sound to associate Chinese cuisine, African hairdos, herbal tea and sex movies with the alienation generation, it nevertheless remains a fact that this generation introduced the paraphernalia of exotic novelties into the menu of our daily life, in which every taste can find its own satisfier. A varied menu does not add up to a lifestyle, however. Rather, certain practices, tastes and preferences constitute *patterns*. One can easily identify several such patterns in which 'this goes with that', but not with something else.

However, a problem presents itself with respect to this infinite variety, this pluralization of the ways of life, this demise of self-complacent and ethnocentric class cultures. Hannah Arendt, and others, have stressed that social classes are necessary for the conduct of rational politics. Classes can give birth to institutions (political organizations which represent their interests). Representative governments grow out of class society. If classes are on the wane, if cultures are becoming pluralized to the degree of total particularization, is a meaningful, rational decision-making process still possible? Only corporations are organized according to functions, and corporations do not represent the interests of ways of life as a whole, but rather the interests of particular functions. Thus, societies based on corporate decision-making can easily be described as 'mass societies', despite cultural pluralization. The 'alienation generation' made a case for 'grassroots politics', for a kind of politics embedded in communities and ways of life on all levels of social stratification. It remains uncertain at this stage whether cultural relativization and pluralization will lead to the demise of rational policy-making or whether they will rather be the prelude to a more democratic and more rational form, or forms, of political action, a combination of the parliamentary system with a type of direct democracy. At this point we do not have sufficient data for extrapolation.

Let us now turn to the change in the intergenerational relations. All three waves of movements were carried by the younger generation. However, the term 'young' requires clarification. In a functional society, 'the young' are those men and women (and not just those boys and girls) who do not perform a 'function' that locks them into one stratum or another within the social division of labour. Thus students are young even when they are thirty years of age, which meant 'middle age' in the generation of our grandparents. Precisely because of this functional connotation, we will in what follows avoid the distinction between 'young' and 'old'. (In any case, old people or 'senior citizens' do not have a job these days. They are, in other words, the 'post-functional ones'.)

The present changes in the relationship of pre-functional and functional generations are so obvious that one can read them from quite external signs. In class-related cultures young men tried hard to look older than their age. After World War Two, however, the pattern gradually transformed to the point where it was, finally, totally reversed. Those who are mentally and physically fully grown up now make sometimes desperate efforts to look like youngsters and behave accordingly. 'Looks' have different social meanings. Looking older than one's age expresses the aspiration to be treated as a responsible adult, as someone who has been settled or at least who is ready for being settled. Looking younger than one's age expresses the aspiration to be treated as someone who is still open to every option, who is not yet a 'bureaucrat', who is not yet fossilized by his/her function. At the peak of generational waves, it has become a common practice that members of the 'functional generation' look for the favours of their children in order to be regarded as 'honorary youth'. The term and the practices of 'mid-life crisis' were invented in this world of the functional division of labour; it is the exclusive production of functional society. In a class culture, be it bourgeois, working class or genteel, being middle-aged lends one a dignity which is the representative quality of the fully-fledged adult. It is *qua* adult, as someone who is *still* able-bodied and -minded but *already* the repository of a great amount of experience, that one becomes a *persona* in a given culture. Men in mid-life crisis wish to be immature and not-yet-settled again, bald teenagers looking for a new identity.

The functional division of labour is attended by a very complex and ambivalent combination. Function performance requires identification, particularly in business, and in public institutions. The stronger the identification with function-performing, the greater the temptation for a person to become a self-complacent bore or an arrogant bureaucrat. The function-performer is almost inevitably driven to lock out young people because they are competition. Function-related self-complacency is often nothing more than a psychological cover-up for the fear of competition. It follows from this that parents of this kind have no major conflict with their own children, as had typically transpired in the dramatic period of generational conflict, but rather with the children of others. Looking young has therefore a double function: it helps the adults to be 'accepted' by the young in their own milieu and it lends them weight in their competition with the children of others. It is precisely this conflict that is normally solved in 'mid-life crisis' when the middle-aged person resigns from competition and dons the costume of the young. The world after World War Two is no longer Oedipal. What other kinds of neurosis it will develop is another matter. Lasch's thesis on narcissism is a significant attempt at exploring our new diseases.

Let us make one final observation about the three waves of cultural movement after World War Two. In all the ups and downs of their continuities and discontinuities, one feature has remained stable. Feminist movements have constituted a major trend in all three, and this is the trend which, despite some minor set-backs, has totally changed modern culture. Feminism was, and has remained, the greatest and most decisive *social* revolution of modernity. Unlike a political revolution, a social revolution does not break out: it takes place. A social revolution is always a cultural revolution as well. The relativization of cultures and the inroads made by 'alien' cultures into western cultures have been repeatedly mentioned above. The feminist revolution is not just one contribution to this enormous change, but the single major one. For female culture, hitherto marginalized and unacknowledged, is now well on its way to articulating a final statement on its own behalf, to claim its half of the traditional culture of humankind. The feminist revolution is not just a novel phenomenon of western culture, *it is a watershed in all hitherto existing cultures*.

The feminist revolution could not have been brought about by the new form of the division of labour alone. Democratic institutions, the value-ideas of freedom, equality and rights had to be present in the global 'imaginary institution of signification' for feminist movements, these carriers of the revolution, to come about. For previously women, just like men, could be incorporated into the functional division of labour, and yet women could also remain subjected to male domination. But without a functional division of labour, the objective of the feminist revolution would have remained unattained for the simplest of reasons: women would not have achieved the opportunity to make a living of their own, to acquire the minimal precondition of an independent life.

Why is it such a widespread belief that 'movements have disappeared', that the past forty years was a period in which 'nothing has happened'? Perhaps because we are too much used to history as political history. And yet history is, first and foremost, social and cultural; it is the history of the daily lives of men and women. Placed under close scrutiny, this history will disclose changes which include a social revolution. The three waves of cultural movement analysed above were the main stewards of this transformation. They did not alter the vessel, but they did change the ocean on which the vessel sails.

11
Europe – An Epilogue?

I

European culture is perhaps the shortest-lived of all cultures in recorded history, or so it would seem.

Culture and the consciousness of culture are coexistent with one another. A consciousness of culture requires the identification of the carrier of culture, a commitment to a particular way of life and a belief in the superiority of that way of life. All of these requirements are met, for example, in the habitual analyses of 'Greek culture': the centre of Hellenism was Greece, the texts read were Homer and other Greek classics, and those who did not wish to practise gymnastics naked were considered barbarian. In a similar fashion, the centre of European culture is allegedly 'Europe'. But since when have we been discussing 'European culture'? Furthermore, who are the discussers? Finally, in what sense is 'European culture' discussed?

A specifically European identity was not formed before the eighteenth century. During this time the patterns of modernity were also put into final shape. The eighteenth century was characterized by specific ongoing changes in its social life, and political imagination, which eventually began to fuse and reinforce each other until they reached the point of no return. The concept 'Europe' (or the west) stood precisely for this brand-new socio-political *dynamis* or 'imaginary institution of social signification' or historical consciousness or form of discourse – the philosophical paradigms we use may vary but the story will remain the same. *Modernity, the creation of Europe itself created Europe*, and this is more than a paradox. The European identity was not a 'natural' one in the same way as one could speak of a Greek, Roman or Jewish identity. For Europe and its history, there was no *ab urbe condita* as such. 'Europe', the mythological figure, which gave its name to the continent, was Greek. The inhabitants of the continent identified themselves as Christians, and for a long time, as Catholic (universal) Christians. Their *urbs* was therefore Jerusalem where the Messiah lived and died as well as Rome, the centre of Christianity. Politically, they understood themselves to be the heirs of the Roman Empire. As far as they had a common language, it was Latin. And when the educated classes stopped speaking Latin, 'Europeans' no longer had a *lingua franca*. The sixteenth and seventeenth centuries were characterized neither by the unification nor by the establishment of a common integration termed 'Europe'. In lieu of the survival of a universalizing humanity, there was rather a nascent, and quickly emerging, diversification and differentiation. Instead of a single Christianity, there were many Christian religions. Nation states began to emerge. National and religious wars decimated and divided the continent. New continents were discovered and populated. Experiments with alternative economic policies and political institutions were launched.

It seems that it was precisely this pluralism, or diversity of experiences and lifestyles producing a sufficient variety of forms, which triggered the combination of the latter into that unique venture we call 'modernity'. 'Modern' indeed appeared as the unity of the manifold. In fact, the allegory of the 'tree', the favourite form of representation of cultures, of their expansion and diversification, provides no illustration for the case of 'Europe'. The soil on which the allegorical tree of 'European culture' was supposed to grow, was in fact never perceived or identified as 'Europe' or 'the west'. Prior to the eighteenth century, no one had been complaining that particular branches of the 'European culture' had been cut from the lifeline of 'the west'. The new world of modernity, the one which came about through the combination of diverse and distinct experiences, discoveries and visions, has been termed 'Europe' or 'the west' only from the eighteenth century onwards. The project 'Europe' in this sense is thus rootless. And, from the very moment of its inception, it has been a project. Modernity is future-orientated, and so is the shared imagination of modern 'European' nations.

Yet there is no cultural self-identity without history. One will not perceive European *culture* without stories and legends *ab urbe condita* which we have once heard from our ancestors, without having learned from our tutors how Europe had been established by gods, demi-gods and heroes; without experiencing in our formative years the 'Other' which is not Europe. For without all of these aspects, there is no European culture. The project termed 'Europe' or 'the west' requires a cultural backing, a brand-new *cultural mythology*. This new cultural mythology is perforce not political in nature for several reasons, the main one being that the west, the project 'Europe', had never been established as a political entity which would have imposed certain common political duties or political obligations. Although the Utopian idea of a United States of Europe emerged relatively early, it was quickly suppressed by vintage nationalism. Political mythologies were bound to strengthen national, rather than 'western' or 'European' identity. Religious mythologies were already occupied, so to speak, in the sense that they were rooted in a non-European tradition, and they could thus enhance a completely new imagination only by entering into the service of national mythologies. At any rate, the European genius is not a religious genius; and in this respect it has always copied and imitated. European identity, or the identity of the west, has been brought into focus by non-identity: the European genius or 'spirit' imagined, projected, and thus created humankind, as well as the other universal notions as 'art' or 'culture'. If there is a humankind, then everyone lives in (a particular kind of) culture, everyone creates (a particular kind of) art. Yet, and this was at the heart of European self-identification, European culture is not simply one among many, but rather the highest, most supreme culture or art, indeed, the overarching one in the cornucopia of diverse cultures and arts. And yet, the recognition of the accomplishments of others has always been part and parcel of the European identity. The myth of occident and orient is not a juxtaposition of civilization to barbarism but rather of one civilization to another. European (western) cultural identity has been conceived of as both ethnocentric and anti-ethnocentric (both terms have been coined by it), as absolutist and relativist, as progressivist and historicist.

European, western, tradition has thus been created retrospectively. Medieval cathedrals, renaissance cities, sacred oratorios and lay sonnets became codified and arranged side by side as manifestations of an entity called 'Europe' or 'the west'. History was re-counted as world history, a holistic narrative the last chapter of which happened to be the history of Europe, the so-called 'newest age'. The invention of the most plausible scenario is Hegel's feat. In terms of this scenario, world history is viewed as the progressive line of events in which every culture made its contribution to evolution, only to later disappear and give way to the new. These successive changes of cultures had only one direction though: progress towards freedom. Modern culture is in fact the realization of freedom for all; this is why it is also the pinnacle and the end result of world history. Hegel's is not a completely evolutionist scenario. Progress was invariably accompanied by losses; old values disappeared and old heroism is now gone. Yet since the yardstick of progress is reason and freedom, and since west-European culture is the most rational and freest of all, the losses need not be weighed against the gains for the former do not matter.

Yet 'Europe' could live in peace with its own self-identity only for the duration of a century, and despite certain trends to the contrary, *the nineteenth century was in the main the century of European culture*. Modernity *alias* the west *alias* Europe was then self-confident. What can be termed 'European culture' thus flourished mainly during the period from the Napoleonic wars to the outbreak of World War One. During this time, the project of modernity succeeded. However, the European genius which created not only a new, but a completely unprecedented socio-political and cultural framework, apparently became exhausted after so great a labour. The twentieth century thus begins with the narrative of the decline of the west. Europeans in increasing numbers began to refer to their own culture as the civilization of a new barbarism. All the great promises of the eighteenth century, the progress of knowledge, technology and freedom now appeared as so many sources of danger and decay and manifestations of decadence. Totalitarian systems growing out of western culture seemed to corroborate the gloomiest diagnoses and predictions. In addition, Europe began to shrink. The real geographic proportions between Europe and the rest of the world gradually began to make themselves felt. The British Empire, one of the last world empires to date, collapsed. This event was of singular importance, in that it was the British Empire that had come closest to the Hellenistic ideal: it modelled the ways of life of its colonial upper classes in the image of the mother country. Because of this drive, English became the Greek (or Latin) of the modern world. Yet European self-identity hardly developed in colonizing Britain. For an English person, Europe meant the Continent, and the island of Britain was a separate world. This attitude began to change only when the Empire ended.

Modernity, the brainchild of 'Europe' invaded the world in all directions. But the world which embraced one or another aspect of the European vision, did not behave in the manner of Hellenistic city-states. Homer and Plato organically belonged to Greek civilization: where Greek civilization went, Homer and Plato followed. Yet Gothic cathedrals, or even Mozart, do not belong to 'the west' or 'Europe' in the same way as Homer and Plato did to the Greek. Wherever modernity ('the west', 'Europe') goes, Mozart does not necessarily follow. For Mozart or Shakespeare are Europeans in a sense completely different from the one in which Homer and Plato were Greek. Together with modernity, 'Europe' created history of a kind which does not allow its self-created cultural tradition to be disseminated together with its real identity: modernity. Indeed, European culture seems to be the shortest-lived of all cultures in recorded human history.

II

The European genius that created modernity developed it to culminate in a point of no return. The project was inherently future-orientated, and, as a result, social phantasy turned toward the future. The fundamental creed became one of progression. Progression appeared to be unlimited. The image of unlimited progression, furthermore, goes with the image of cumulation. Since not every kind of knowledge and experience is cumulative, the European imagination was directed towards those kinds of knowledge which were, such as the knowledge which could be accumulated in the natural sciences and technology. Technological imagination, that is, the pursuit of cumulative 'know-how' and 'know-what' is undoubtedly one of the fundaments of modern civilization. Yet, as Collingwood so presciently remarked, experience in statecraft can also be cumulative. Modern men and women began to experiment with entirely new and unprecedented forms of power and rule. In fact, it took a remarkably short amount of time to establish such novel forms of power and rule as constitutional monarchy, liberal democracy, totalitarian democracy (Jocobinism), totalitarianism pure and simple as well as an amazing number of variations within each type. Modern states hardly have any organic roots. They are artefacts of 'statecraft', and learning processes in the service of the problem-solving mind for better or worse. Never since the period when the Greeks invented the city-state, the *polis*, has there been so much energy and ingenuity invested in conjuring up institutions of human coexistence and co-operation. This new creative energy can, furthermore, be invested in institutionalizing freedom on a hitherto unknown level. Greek democracy, the Roman republic, medieval liberties of estates and free cities, ancient parliaments – each of these formations offered a particular model and lent themselves to combination and experimentation. In this way, the ancient political heritage has been incorporated into the identity called 'European culture'. And it was this way that moderns learned to mix forms of personal freedom with specially designed bodies of collective decision-making. Parallel with accumulation of technological know-how and that of the experience of political 'craftmanship' went the accumulation of wealth on the one hand, and poverty on the other. Thus, the three processes of accumulation and discovery which together make up western, or 'European' culture may be identified as industrialization, capitalism and the statecraft of the modern nation states. All three elements can spread, all three are designed to be exported, and thus are no longer exclusively European. It should be added that totalitarianism, the power of absolute control is as much a European invention as liberal democracy. If totalitarianism spreads, the west, or 'Europe' is in this sense exported with it.

Seen from this perspective, the 'western', or 'European', imagination prevailed as a universalizing power. Not even ethnocentrism and anti-ethnocentrism, these twins of a short-lived western tradition appear from this angle as mere contradictions or opposing trends. European universalism, the absolutist scenario, proved to be a realistic project, for every nation of the world was included by it into a modernizing universe. And similarly, relativism also became a realistic attitude because it transpired that concrete cultural traditions may remain unaffected by the modern project, and that the latter can go together with any culture whatsoever. In the final analysis, distinct cultures are all alike, for while none of them can resist the victorious power of accumulation, each of them can remain unaffected while being embraced by the accumulation process.

The cumulative phantasy, the open horizon of unlimitedness, permeates western thought, creativity and need-structure in all its pores. Each day something new must be created; the product of yesterday is unfit for today. There is nothing natural in the speed with which art forms become antiquated. It is rather the result of the intrusion of (mainly technological) problem-solving in the sphere of arts, problem-solving which, once those problems are solved, raises new ones to be solved all over again. Yet the 'newer' product is no more beautiful or meaningful than the earlier one was. What happens is simply that the earlier one becomes 'unacceptable', and as such, occupies a place in the museum called Europe. The unrepeatability of style, rather than the inimitableness of the individual work, results from the cumulative attitude. However, whereas in technology the scope, the forms, and the attainable variations of new inventions are not exhausted, within the sphere of forms of artistic or philosophical imagination, the sphere which Hegel referred to as 'the absolute spirit', forms can indeed be exhausted. Sensual experience is the anthropological limit which reduces the available number of forms of sensual pleasure through artistic experience and beauty. If problem-solving runs amok, limits to artistic experience can easily be reached. Twelve-tone technique in music has proved a cul-de-sac precisely for this reason. The 'ever-new' vision had to return to the old, the oldest, the other and the alien in order to cope with this quandary. The treasure-house of every culture on earth had to be plundered in order to reach sham-accumulation, when in fact there was none. The current predilection with quotation and pastiche may be understood against this backdrop. For the term 'quotation' only makes sense where novelty is the expectation, and where the emphasis on ever-new forms of problem-solving in arts becomes a taken-for-granted practice. Philosophy undergoes a similar process of 'roll-forward'. For philosophy is the genre of rendering meaning and of speculative thought rather than a genre of cumulative knowledge. If the limits of genre are trespassed, the result will be destruction rather than progression. However, it also goes without saying that cumulative vision affects different genres of art in different ways. The more authentically technical problems are involved in a genre, the more cumulative vision can become fertilizing and vice versa.

While morality itself is not cumulative, the ethical attitude can be. Kant once expressed his hope that certain kinds of institutions could be established within which even the race of devils would behave decently. Ethics, particularly political ethics, has two cumulative aspects. First, learning from the failure of particular institutions, establishing new ones or correcting the shortcomings of the old can be cumulative; and, second, the same applies to learning decent public behaviour. As mentioned, our modern world proved extremely creative in inventing institutions. The nineteenth century, the century of European-western culture, invented liberal democracy, universal suffrage, trade unions, party politics and so much more. At no time prior to modernity had the lower classes participated in shaping the lives of their respective community, excepting the forms of supplication and violent rebellion. The class struggles which ravaged the great

European century, brought with them the unexpected yield that from then on, institutional and ethical know-how showed an unmistakable trend of accumulation in every social stratum.

There is, however, an internal contradiction which exists between the two aspects of accumulating institutional experience. Inventing ever-new institutions or addressing ourselves to the reform of the old ones, goes hand in hand with a future-directed, cumulative imaginary. Yet the habit of acting in the spirit of already existing institutions requires a different kind of cumulative capacity; and the second capacity may be at odds with the first. Certain institutions must be legitimized as stable, and therefore untouchable, corner-stones of political life for the second type of accumulation to come about. Yet in modernity, only those institutions can be stabilized which allow for accumulating political experience as well as for continuous appeals to greater social and political justice. Of the political forms invented in modernity, only that one which combines liberalism and democracy, can live up to such expectations.

The century of Europe from the American and French Revolutions to the end of World War One did invent certain forms of liberal democracy, but it did not generalize them even in Europe itself. And this is rather an understatement. Torn by class division and class war, Europe became once again the battlefield of nations on an unprecedented scale. The new institutions proved frail, in that they did not provide ethics and public morals and there was no tradition behind them. As a result of this inherent frailty, they were swept away by institutionalized un-freedom. Knowledge was accumulated further and further, as were wealth, the experience of totalitarianism and the technologies of warfare. As Ortega y Gasset warned: barbarism emerged as the outcome of European civilization. And Europe was finally cleared from European barbarism by exclusively non-European forces, among them by a civilized barbarism of still another kind. Cumulative imagination has swept through the world. Modernity is no longer European. Technological imagination primarily flourishes these days on the coast of the Pacific Ocean, and Europeans have begun to learn certain political lessons from their own early modern product, the United States.

III

Collingwood was the first to dismiss the question of whether we are 'progressive' or 'decadent' as a completely irrelevant one. For the answer depends on one's criterion of progression (and regression) and therefore on our own point of view. If we measure progression by the standards of 'accumulation', there can be no doubt whatsoever that a long-term progression had transpired in Europe. Western and central Europe is certainly more wealthy than it used to be and, more importantly, it can be argued that the distribution of wealth has become more equitable. The 'social state', the creation of social democracy, has expanded our vision of accumulation to including 'general standards of living' in the appraisal: a certain level of poverty is perceived as a socially intolerable phenomenon. With the exception of a certain part of east-central Europe, liberal democracies of different kinds have begun to take root, some of them still new and fragile. Since it is highly unlikely that liberal democracies will fight a war against each other, western-south-eastern Europe seems to be protected from the types of national conflict which may result in re-barbarization and destruction. Traditional national hatreds are subdued and a degree of co-operation beween the nations has once again become possible.

At the same time, the theory of 'decadence' can also rely on a certain amount of empirical evidence. For, as mentioned, the genius of Europe seems to be exhausted after so exacting a labour. Despite the obvious exaggerations of *Kulturkritik*, there are unmistakable symptoms of an impoverished creative phantasy, of the mass production of a confectioned imagination, of learned stupidity and professional narrow-mindedness, loss of meanings and meaningful practices when compared to the past. If imagination centres on mass production, the mass production of imagination is unavoidable. In addition, Europe embarked on a crash course of relativizing its own culture so much that it arrived at a stage of advanced cultural masochism. The most apparent symptom is however the compartmentalization of the once universal future-directed and cumulative phantasy. Apart from the technological version, there is no longer a future-orientated social phantasy in the lands of Europe. Grand narratives of another, better, future in politics, social questions or anything else are no longer forged there. Redemption is deemed undesirable, and socio-political progress ridiculed. Is this still a future-orientated, cumulative world? The old Europe resembles a corpse whose hair and nails, wealth and cumulative knowledge, are still growing, but the rest is dead. It would be absurd to deny that decent philosophy or high-quality works of art are still created on European soil. Although these days the most attractive literature is produced on the so-called peripheries rather than in Europe, once considered the centre, in philosophy, however, the European hegemony has remained uncontested. Yet European nations rather focus their attention on preserving the past and cultivating the traditions. Old cities are rebuilt, ancient castles are refurbished, old artefacts are exhibited, old books are republished – Europeans tiptoe in their cities as museums *because they are museums*. This is also accumulation of a kind because accumulation of knowledge and wealth, the latter in a literal sense, is one of the powerful motifs behind the trendy past-orientatedness. More importantly, the quest for meaning now has a recourse to the past because it is in the past that a meaningful way of life can be fathomed; the present does not provide one. Culture, as Europeans understand it, is a way of life and if they search for it in the past amidst growing nostalgia, then culture as a whole is attached to the past. This is undoubtedly an admission of defeat: European culture turned out to be life without culture in the very interpretation of European culture itself. Viewed from this perspective, European culture can legitimately be considered the cadaver of its own self-image.

Worse still, the meaningful past which is now being constantly unearthed, restored, refurbished, re-made, and rehabilitated is far from being the past of Europe. Europe, lest we forget, was created as an ideal entity in the eighteenth century, and the collectors' frenzy reaches far earlier than that age. It is not the common roots of modernity, the brainchild of Europe, which is now being rediscovered, not even the memorabilia of the modern nation states, but rather something which is hidden deeper in the well of time. The quest is not conducted for the roots of the 'tree of Europe', for these roots never existed, and modern Europeans have only now come to realize that their 'European culture' projected into the remote past is the myth of the nineteenth century. Europe as a museum is not the museum of Europe. The time has perhaps come for a funeral oration.

IV

Yet before we prepare ourselves for the funeral oration, we must first find out what we are going to lay in the grave. We must also find out who the gravedigger is.

Let us recapitulate the self-created mythology of 'Europe'. Once upon a time a young continent, Europe, took over the baton from the defunct Roman Empire. Europe created a culture of its own, and grew different branches on the tree of its culture, which turned out to be the most supreme culture of the whole of recorded history. Commander of the world, it also civilized it, imprinting all other nations, tribes and continents with its own image. The self-created mythology of Europe is of course more than sheer mythology. As long as men and women believe in the story, it has the ring of truth. And in so far as we subscribe to this story, we indeed have to prepare for the funeral oration. Europe, the mighty, the leader of the world, no longer exists; Europe, the source of inspiration for all higher cultures has been exhausted. May it rest in peace.

But we may recount a completely different story and if it makes sense, there is no corpse to be buried. For the entity which seemed to lie in state has not died, because it has never lived. The entity we are about to bury has a different name: modernity. European culture *is* modernity, and modernity is not dead but alive and kicking, whether we like it or not. Indeed, Europe succeeded in imprinting its culture on the whole world in so far as it imprinted its vision on this world. It imprinted the vision of cumulative knowledge, above all, technological know-how, of cumulative wealth, daring to experiment with completely new, and equally cumulative, political forms on the whole world. It also imprinted on the world the forceful power machine of the nation state and the ideology of nationalism as much as the universal ideas of freedom, equality and fraternity. The whole world learns nowadays what Europeans practised so successfully a century ago: the implementation of ideological devices, and the manipulation of the crowd for the national interest via universalistic slogans. At the same time, the whole world also learns the reverse side of the coin; namely the truth that ideas are not empty words and that they can be turned against the ruler, just as the rulers turn them against those they oppress. No culture was ever disseminated so fast, was appropriated so easily, as the 'common European' for the reason that *it was a culture without culture*.

Modernity, European culture *par excellence* is not ready for burial. In Europe itself it has finally settled in comfortably. Functional division of labour, a society which is stratified and rests on conflicting interests but which is also classless, a state which can become corporatist but also democratic to a greater degree than ever before – these are the terms of this settlement. The perception of the demise of modernity that surrounds this state of affairs results from the circumstance that *modernity had already developed its categories*. It is still in motion but does not cross its boundaries. Europe's expansive dynamic has come to a halt for a new framework is now set, and a newer framework is not yet in sight. This is the condition that certain Europeans termed *post-histoire*. The term is a misnomer. Contemporary Europe is 'after-history' only in so far as one accepts the mythology of European identity at its face value, only if one shares the belief that modernity was the last, the highest attainable peak as well as the coronation of a long history of the entity 'Europe'. Since we are after *this* history, we are also after History. But there is a different story still.

Modernity cannot be buried for it never died; rather, it simply worked out its own determinations. Europe, European culture, the European tradition and the like cannot be buried because it never existed. Mythological heroes and demi-gods are not buried. Let us briefly repeat the alternative story. Once upon a time there was at Christian umbrella culture on this tiny continent. This umbrella culture encompassed a host of different tribes, peoples, languages and forms of life. This spot of the world had four interesting and distinctive features. One of them was the division of power prevailing there (between Pope and Emperor). The second was that several separate cultures living alike under the same umbrella were equal in cultural power; thus neither of them could assimilate the others. The third was that a great diversity thronged on a relatively small spot. And the fourth interesting and distinctive feature was the survival among them of the *polis*, the city-state. How the happy coincidence of such diverse factors resulted in the colourful mosaic of premodern European cultures (in the plural) and how they produced together the highest single accomplishment in certain artistic genres, is not our task to try to recount here.

Even if we add them together, European cultures (in the plural) do not add up to 'European culture'. They were cultures in conflict, competition or sometimes simply neglectful of one another. There is Italian and German music, there is Florentine and Venetian painting but there is no European music and no European painting. There is no European drama but there is Shakespeare and the *tragédie classique*. There is no European novel but there is the English, French and Russian novel – for not even the culture of the nineteenth century became 'European culture'. The truth content of this statement is easily verified. What did European nations export to their colonies? The abstractions 'European painting', 'European music' or 'European novel'? All of them exported religion, statecraft, economies, technology – all of which, with the exception of religion to some degree, were ingredients of modernity. And culturally they never exported 'Europe' but what was their own. The British exported golf, cricket, horse racing, clubs and Kipling. The French exported cuisine, linguistic consciousness, fashion and Victor Hugo. Who has ever exported 'European culture' apart from the European brainchild: modernity?

But if modernity did not die, then the gravediggers should be brought to a halt. And how about an epilogue? An epilogue is unlike a funeral oration; it is apposite after the drama came to conclusion. Is there then time for an epilogue?

V

It is difficult to determine when a historical drama comes to an end and when a new drama begins. Whether the celebrated 'eighteenth of Brumaire' is an epilogue or a prologue, depends entirely on the story we are about to tell. Contemporary western Europe looks like the spot where the greatest drama is over. Modernity was created there, it went through several convulsions and now it seems to have come to a halt. It is highly unlikely that 'Europe' will be the initiator of a new imaginary institution of signification, a completely new discourse and the like. And yet, *post-histoire* is still a misnomer, for the term equates history with the *eruption* of a new discourse, of a radically new type of imagination. But, to misquote Kuhn, a history like this is 'revolutionary', not normal, history. And normal history is also history. Slowing down is not tantamount to standing still. Ancient civilizations lasted from eight hundred to two thousand years. Let us be cautious: the revolutionary eruption of the nineteenth, the 'European' century has infected us with a fraudulent sense of temporality. After the drama an epic may follow, not perforce the epilogue.

Yet, *post-histoire*, much as it is a misnomer, does express a changed perception of temporality. So does the term 'postmodern'. If modernity is the drama of permanent revolution, postmodernity may be characterized as the epic of settling-in. And it is more than a simple comfortable arrangement. The Augean stables need to be cleaned. Furthermore, whether the age of epic begins or that of the drama resumes, does not depend solely on Europe. In the arena Europe is now but one of the players.

It would be short sighted to write an epilogue to European culture and history, for European history only begins in the nineteenth century. European people may be old but 'Europe' is still young. 'European culture' which as such never existed, could still develop in the future. This is the first time in the history of the continent when the nations of Europe – the Soviet Union and its sphere of influence still excluded – resigned warring, conquest and territorial expansion. For them, the tradition of the Other became attractive rather than repulsive. Common movements emerge. 'Cultural exchange' still remains on the surface but gradually it may reach deeper layers. What has been designated here as a possible 'new European culture' is not meant as a merger of culture, more of a loss than a gain, rather a new lay umbrella culture in whose framework local, partial and national cultures may thrive. An authentic new European culture does not necessarily contain the *promesse de bonheur*, the advent of a new Shakespeare or a new Mozart. For no human effort or industriousness can willfully produce the happy constellation for the genius, this 'favourite of nature' as Kant put it, to be born. What a new European framework does promise is the emergence of civic virtue, taste, the education of sense, civility, urbanity, joy, nobility, forms of life borne with dignity, sensitivity for nature, manufactured or preserved, as well as poetry, music, drama, painting, piety and erotic culture and so much else. Furthermore, what is asserted here about a future European culture, can be asserted about every possible future cultural framework.

No prologue can be written to a dream; a dream is much too subjective to allow for a public genre. But those sharing the 'European dream' certainly cannot write an epilogue. Their dream still might come true.

Index

Index by Mandy Crook